MARATHON KINGS

D1807877

MARATHON KINGS

PELHAM BOOKS

FOREWORD

© Winchmore Publishing Services
Limited 1983

All rights reserved. No part of this
publication may be reproduced,
stored in a retrieval system, or
transmitted, in any form or by any
means, electronic, mechanical,
photocopying, recording or
otherwise, without the prior
permission of the publisher.

British Library Cataloguing in
Publication Data
Giller, Norman
    The marathon kings.
    1. Marathon running—
        Biography
    I. Title
    796.4'26'0922   GV1065

ISBN 0 7207 1453 2

First Published in Great Britain by
Pelham Books Ltd
44 Bedford Square
London WC1B 3DU
1983

Produced by Winchmore
Publishing Services Limited
40 Triton Square
London NW1
England

Designed by Roy Williams
Edited by Sue Butterworth
Index by Susan Piquemal
Picture research by Malcolm
Rowley
Typeset by SX Composing Limited

Printed and bound by
Graficromo s.a., Cordoba, Spain

More than any other race, the marathon has captured the imagination and interest of the public and athletes alike. It has transcended sport and has become almost a family festival, with gatherings all around the world where thousands of people are brought together by the common bond of the marathon challenge. In this well researched book, *The Marathon Kings*, Norman Giller traces the history and the highlights of the event and gives flesh and blood to what have previously been skeletal statistics. My personal best over the marathon course was 2h 15:49·0. I was pleased with the time, but even more pleased to complete the race. My feeling of achievement as I crossed the finishing line was a satisfying experience known to everybody who has ever mastered the marathon, regardless of the time taken to cover the 26 miles 385 yards. Anybody who finishes a marathon is a winner. *The Marathon Kings* concentrates on the elite of the event, the men and the women who have proved they have no equal on the road. They are a race apart and fully deserve the star treatment that this book gives them.

BRENDAN FOSTER MBE★

*Brendan Foster was Britain's most popular and successful athlete of the 1970s. He was a world record holder at 3,000 metres and 2 miles, European champion over 5,000 metres, European record holder and Olympic bronze medallist at 10,000 metres, Olympic recorder holder at 5,000 metres and Commonwealth Games 10,000 metres champion. His track exploits inspired his home town of Gateshead to become one of the world's most athletics-conscious communities. He is now a respected member of the BBC-TV athletics commentary team and an energetic joint Managing Director of the British wing of the flourishing sportswear company, Nike International.

INTRODUCTION

EMIL ZATOPEK

WALDEMAR CIERPINSKI

CONTENTS

SPIRIDON LOUIS

DORANDO PIETRI

HANNES KOLEHMAINEN

SAM FERRIS

JIM PETERS

ABEBE BIKILA

DEREK CLAYTON

FRANK SHORTER

ALBERTO SALAZAR

ROBERT DE CASTELLA

GRETE WAITZ

THE WINNERS

ARRIVÉE

INTRODUCTION

THE MARATHON USED TO BE CONSIDERED the private territory of cranks and eccentrics. Now it has become the property of the people, with literally tens of thousands brought to their feet for what they regard as the ultimate sporting challenge: to finish a marathon.

This book is about the best of the marathon runners; a history of the kings and queens of the road who have proved themselves a step ahead of all other marathoners. The lure of the marathon is that everybody who finishes the torture trail covering 26 miles 385 yards is a winner. Whether their time is close to two hours, four hours or six hours, they have a sense of achievement known to mountaineers who reach the summit. While in the following pages I have concentrated on the exploits of the marathon champions, I consider everybody who tackles and conquers the marathon course a hero or a heroine. And it is to the running masses that I dedicate this book.

Anybody who doubts that the marathon craze is here to stay may be swayed by these facts: in 1969 in the United States there were just 44 marathons; by the 1980s 200 more had been added to the calendar. In 1979 in Britain there were just 21 marathons; in 1982 the total staged was 116.

It is the 'Big City' runs that have transformed the marathon from an athletics event into a moving festival. Organisers of the major marathons have their biggest headache turning people away from their races. The New York City Marathon, organised by the New York Road Runners Club, attracted just 126 runners in 1970. Club President Fred Lebow had to spend $1,000 out of his own pocket to pay administration costs. Twelve years later 25,000 people applied for the 15,000 places on the starting line and the redoubtable Fred Lebow negotiated a $750,000 contract with ABC for coast-to-coast television coverage of the race. More than 2 million New Yorkers line the route to cheer and encourage the competitors, making every one of them feel a winner. 'People get cheered who have never been cheered in their lives before,' says Fred Lebow. 'They are overwhelmed by what becomes a mutual feeling of love and affection.'

Chris Brasher, 1956 Olympic steeplechase gold medallist who played such a prominent part in Roger Bannister's first four minute mile run, was one of the competitors who experienced the New York 'love in' when he ran in the 1979 race. In an inspired article in *The Observer*, he wrote: 'To believe this story, you must believe that the human race can be one joyous family, working together, laughing together, achieving the im-

Facing page: An artist's impression of Frenchman Michel Theato winning the 1900 Olympic title in Paris. Above: A long, long trail awinding for the runners in the 1982 New York Marathon.

Big City marathons were a hundred years away when this drawing (*left*) appeared in a French magazine to depict the torture of long-distance running. But it's difficult to experience the loneliness of the long-distance runner in modern marathons like the New York classic (*below left*).

possible. I believe it because I saw it happen. Last Sunday, in one of the most violent, trouble-stricken cities in the world, 11,532 men, women and children from 40 countries of the world, assisted by 2·5 million black, white and yellow people, Protestants and Catholics, Jews and Muslims, Buddhists and Confucians, laughed, cheered and suffered during the greatest folk festival the world has seen.'

Brasher had been bitten – incurably – by the marathon bug and he was determined to become 'a carrier'. He passed the bug on to his readers with this teasing challenge: 'I wonder whether London could stage such a festival? We have the course, a magnificent course. But do we have the heart and hospitality to welcome the world?'

He then provided action to go with his words and set about organising a London Marathon. With £50,000 sponsorship backing from Gillette and the support of the Greater London Council and the police, the resolute Brasher was in a position by October 1980 to announce that there would be a London Marathon the following March. Brasher confidentally predicted that the record British field of 750 would be exceeded. What he did not expect was to be flooded by 21,000 entries. Marathon Madness had hit Britain.

The field for the inaugural London Marathon was limited to 7,055 starters of which all but 637 finished. There was an international flavour to the race with American Dick Beardsley and the Norwegian Inge Simonsen running a friendly dead-heat for first place in 2h 11:48·0, then the fastest time recorded in an English marathon. Fred Lebow, mastermind of the New York

Marathon 'Madness' hit London in 1981 (*below*) with 7,055 starters in Chris Brasher's 'dream' race. It finished with a sporting dead-heat between American Dick Beardsley and Norwegian Inge Simonsen (*right*) that captured the friendly spirit of the event.

classic, competed in the London event with the number 0001. 'In many respects it surpassed New York,' he said. 'Londoners can be extremely proud. It took us a decade to get to the sort of crowd turn-out that this race had. The organisation was top class and the friendliness of the spectators proved that the marathon brings out the best in people. There was a marvellous spirit out there on the road right from start to finish.'

By 1982 the London Marathon – 'Brasher's Dream' – had mushroomed to a point where there were 16,350 starters and twice that number were turned away.

In the United States alone, it is estimated that in the 1980s more than 30 million people were pounding the roads in a search for fitness and achievement. Road running has become big business for the shoe and sportswear industry and alleged under-the-counter payments to amateurs has triggered a lot of controversy, but 99 per cent of marathoners still do it purely for the sheer satisfaction, fun and better mental and physical health that they derive from long-distance running.

Emil Zatopek, the legendary Olympic hero, summed up marathon running when he said: 'If you want to run, then run a mile. If you want to experience another life, run a marathon.' And Tom McNab, distinguished athletics coach, author of *Flanagan's Run* and technical adviser on *Chariots of Fire*, commented during the 1982 New York marathon: 'In marathon running, there's only one race – and that's the human race.'

His statement captures why the marathon has become the greatest race on earth. This book is a salute to the elite of the event, the kings and queens of the road.

Norman Giller
Thorpe Bay, Essex
January 1983

SPIRIDON LOUIS

THE GREEK MESSENGER WHO DELIVERED THE FIRST OLYMPIC MARATHON VICTORY

ACCORDING TO GREEK LEGEND it was a soldier called Pheidippides who started it all in the year 490 BC. The Greek army had fought off an invasion by Persian forces at Marathon, a battle plain some 25 miles north-east of Athens. Pheidippides, an Olympic champion runner, was dispatched on foot to carry the news of the victory to the people of Athens. He ran all the way and had only enough breath left on arrival to gasp, 'Rejoice, we conquer', before dropping down dead in the town centre.

The idea of a marathon race came some 2,386 years later. It was the brainchild of Frenchman Michel Bréal, a student of Greek mythology who suggested that a race along the Marathon-Athens route taken by Pheidippides would make a fitting climax to the revival of the Olympic Games in Athens in 1896.

It became a matter of national pride that Greece should provide the winner of the inaugural running of the marathon and a nationwide search was launched for competitors. After a series of eliminating races, they found 21 would-be champions ready to follow in the footsteps of the heroic Pheidippides.

Among them was a former Greek shepherd, Spiridon Louis, who after army service had become a post office messenger. He used to build up his stamina by running alongside his mules while delivering letters and barrels of water to outlying districts on the Marathon-Athens route. All kinds of inducements were offered to inspire the Greek entrants to try to win the race. Some were outrageous such as the million drachmas plus the hand of his daughter in marriage offered by Georgios Averoff, the chief benefactor of the revived Games.

There were also offers of a lifetime's free supply of clothes, wine, chocolate, bread, shaves and haircuts, and gifts of cattle, sheep and jewelry.

There were four foreign competitors in the field of 25 starters: Frenchman Albin Lermusiaux, Hungarian

Facing page: Spiridon Louis, clutching the first of his many gifts after his win in 1896.

Above: Spiridon Louis, the hero of Athens.

LOUIS

Three Greek competitors train for the first ever Olympic marathon (*right*) and later line up at the start (*below*) at the bridge of Marathon.

Facing page: An artist's impression of the finish of the 1896 marathon, with Prince George accompanying Spiridon Louis across the line.

Gyula Kellner, American Arthur Blake – second in the 1,500 metres – and Australian Edwin Flack, who was attempting an ambitious treble after winning both the 800 and 1,500 metres on the track.

Spiridon Louis was satisfied that he had made the proper preparations for the race. He had fasted the day before and spent long hours on the last two nights in deep prayer.

The first ever Olympic marathon was started from the bridge of Marathon at 2 pm. Accompanying the runners on horseback were Greek soldiers who cleared the path ahead of the thousands of spectators lining the route. Bringing up the rear in horsedrawn carts was a team of doctors and nurses.

As a single pistol shot signalled the start, Frenchman Lermusiaux set off at a suicidal pace and with less than a third of the race run he was nearly a mile ahead of the rest of the field led by Flack and Blake. After being prematurely crowned as the inevitable winner by excited spectators, Lermusiaux collapsed in exhaustion with more than an hour's running between him and the finish in Athens. Flack and Blake were now in the lead and Greek supporters urged Louis to step up his pace in third place. He stopped at a pre-arranged point to drink half a pint of wine and told spectators: 'Everything is going to plan. My turn will come yet.' Blake and then Flack, both choked by the dust being kicked up by the escort of soldiers on their horses, dropped out and the jogging, fresh-looking Louis was out on his own for the last three miles. As he entered the stadium in Athens to

a tumultuous roar from the crowd, Prince George and Crown Prince Constantine raced from the Royal Box to join him on the final lap to the finishing tape.

Louis, at 25, became a Greek hero on the same scale as Pheidippides but he lived to enjoy his fame and he was showered with gifts that made him comfortably well off for the rest of his life. The one offer he turned down was marriage to Miss Averoff. He was already a married man with two children.

Greek runners filled five of the first six places with the Hungarian Kellner being awarded a special bronze medal as the first (and only) overseas runner to finish the race. He came in fourth but was promoted to third after the Greek who finished just ahead of him had been disqualified for taking a lift in a horse-drawn carriage. Kellner's time was 3h 06:35·0. Louis won in 2h 58:50·0, the only man to finish the course inside 3 hours.

Americans competing in Athens carried stories of the marathon dramas back to the United States and the idea was taken up in Boston and New York. The New York City Knickerbocker Athletic Club introduced a marathon into their annual programme on 20 September 1896 – just five months after the first Olympic marathon. The course was a challenging, hilly 25-mile run from Stamford, Connecticut, to the Columbia Oval track in New York. Thirty runners set out on roads saturated by torrential rain and conditions were so

Louis gets the 'Royal' treatment after his triumph as he poses with a parade of Greek princes.

The veteran Louis (*above*) is accompanied by Hitler's aide after being introduced to the German dictator during the 1936 Olympics.

Below: The runners set off from the Parc des Princes at the start of the 1900 Olympic marathon in Paris.

treacherous that the pace was slow. New Yorkers John McDermott and Hamilton Gray battled for the lead, with McDermott unleashing a powerful finish to win in just under 3h 30.

The famous Boston Athletic Club was next to stage a marathon to celebrate Patriot's Day on 19 April 1897. Huge crowds lined the route and often impeded the progress of the runners with carriages and wagons. Once again it was McDermott and Gray who set the pace and McDermott fought off an attack of cramp to go away and win by nearly 7 minutes. Subsequent New York and Boston marathons were superbly organised, which could not be said of the 1900 Olympic marathon in Paris.

Michel Théato, a Parisian baker's roundsman, knew all the ins-and-outs and short cuts of the back streets of Paris and it was strongly suspected that he had used some of them on his way to victory. American Arthur Newton was convinced he had won the race. He claimed that he had taken the lead just after the halfway stage and that nobody had overtaken him from then until the finish line. Newton, who had proved himself one of the world's greatest long-distance runners over the previous two years, could not believe it when he was told he had come in fifth, more than 30 minutes behind Théato.

Another American, Dick Grant, later brought an unsuccessful lawsuit against the International Olympic Committee. He alleged that a cyclist had knocked him down as he was making a challenge for the lead. The race was poorly signposted and there was no marshalling of the crowds of sightseers. Twelve of the 19 starters gave up in a mixture of despair and exhaustion. Swedish competitor Ernst Fast did the obvious thing when he got lost on the marathon route. He stopped and asked a policeman the way. Fast was pointed in the

wrong direction and completely lost touch with the leaders. There was so much controversy over the incident that the unfortunate policeman involved later shot himself in a fit of depression. It was 12 years before Théato was finally confirmed as the official winner of the race.

Thomas Hicks, born in Birmingham, England, but representing the United States, won the St Louis marathon at the 1904 Olympics but not before a hoaxer had been hailed as the champion. Fred Lorz had dropped out of the race after 9 miles because of severe cramp and gratefully accepted a lift to the stadium. The automobile in which he was travelling broke down and so Lorz completed the last 4 miles on foot. When he came trotting into the stadium way ahead of marathon leader Hicks the crowd rose to acclaim Lorz, thinking he was the winner. He did nothing to disillusion them and allowed himself to be carried in triumph to the VIP area of the stadium where he was introduced to Alice Roosevelt, the daughter of the President. He was about to be presented with the gold medal when officials who had been accompanying Hicks stopped the presentation and exposed Lorz as an imposter.

It was later announced that Lorz had been banned from athletics for life, but his explanation that he had been having a joke that got out of hand was accepted. He won the American marathon championship the following year without any motorised assistance.

Judging by today's strictly applied rules of the road in marathon running, Hicks himself would have been disqualified. He was in a state of near collapse for the last third of the race and was kept going by the administration of strychnine tablets, raw eggs and brandy. At one stage two spectators supported him as he weaved around on rubber legs and his coach hosed him down with water taken from a car radiator. He finished the 40 kilometre (24·86 mile) race at walking pace and collapsed unconscious after crossing the finish line.

It was only after he was discharged from hospital that he was awarded his medal. He never ran the marathon again. The race was run in blistering heat, with temperatures a scorching 90° in the shade. Seventeen of the 31 runners failed to finish the demanding course and two South African competitors were chased three-quarters of a mile off course by a ferocious dog.

The most fascinating and unfortunate character in the 1904 race was Felix Carvajal, a postman from Cuba, who raised his boat fare to the United States by giving running exhibitions in the centre of Havana and then going around the gathered crowds for donations.

During the boat trip, he had his luggage stolen and lost all his money in a dice game. The tiny, 5 ft Cuban had to hitch his way from New Orleans to St Louis. He turned up for the race wearing walking shoes, long trousers and a long-sleeved shirt. American discus thrower Martin Sheridan felt sorry for him because everybody was laughing at his expense and so he borrowed a pair of shears and trimmed his sleeves and trouser legs to make him at least look the part of an athlete.

Carvajal, running his first ever marathon, was giving a good account of himself and was in with a victory chance until he came across a fruit orchard. He stopped and started stuffing himself with apples and peaches. The fruit was not ripe and poor Felix spent much of the next hour ducking in and out of bushes trying to overcome stomach problems. He finally managed to finish a creditable fourth.

At an interim Olympics in Athens in 1906, Canadian Bill Sherring covered the original Marathon-Athens course in 2h 51:23·6, with Sweden's John Svanberg also beating the 3-hour barrier in second place.

The following year, Thomas Longboat – a Canadian Indian teenager – won the Boston marathon at faster than 6-minute miling pace. He looked a certainty for future Olympic honours but turned to professional running and set a world record over 15 miles in Toronto in 1912. The pace he set when winning the Boston marathon would have taken him to victory in the 1948 Olympics, and certainly in the 1908 Games when the marathon really arrived in the world spotlight.

Canadian Bill Sherring takes the last lap of the 1906 interim Olympics marathon in his stride.

Right: Thomas Longboat, the Canadian Indian whose tribal name was Deerfoot.

DORANDO PIETRI

THE CANDYMAN FROM CAPRI WHO BECAME AN OLYMPIC HERO IN DEFEAT

THE SUN WAS SCORCHING DOWN from a cloudless blue sky at 2.30 pm on Friday, 24 July 1908, when 54 competitors set out from Windsor Castle on a 26-mile marathon run to the White City. Once they reached the stadium they would have just another 385 yards to negotiate around the cinder track to cross the finish line in front of the Royal Box, where Queen Alexandra was waiting to greet the winner. Thus it was that the marathon distance became standardised throughout the world at 26 miles 385 yards (42·195 km).★ Those extra 385 yards proved to be the bridge too far for Dorando Pietri, a slim little candymaker from Capri in Italy.

Dorando, a comical looking figure in his white vest and red knickerbockers, overtook South African favourite Charles Hefferon with two miles to go and was comfortably in the lead when he reached the stadium. But the sweltering conditions that had already forced 29 of the runners out of the race suddenly took their toll on the Italian and he slowed to what looked like a drunken walk as he came on to the track in front of a roaring, capacity crowd. He turned right instead of left, tottered and crumpled slowly to the ground like a puppet that has had its strings cut away.

Doctors and track officials crowded anxiously around him as he was helped to his feet and then pointed and pushed in the right direction for the finishing tape. Four times Dorando collapsed and each time helping hands – including those of Sherlock Holmes creator Sir Arthur Conan Doyle – reached out to rescue him from his sea of despair. Finally, with the

crowd urging and willing the near-unconscious Italian to victory, he staggered across the line, supported on both sides by well-meaning officials.

Opposite: The most famous or infamous finish in Olympic history as the exhausted Dorando is helped through the tape.

Above: Dorando (No 19) is an early pace-setter as the field leaves Windsor Castle.

★Although the distance is standardised there are no officially recognised records for the marathon because of the varying courses and conditions.

PIETRI

The drama of the 'Dorando Marathon' captured by the camera:

Above: Two cycling attendants encourage Dorando as he crosses tramlines at Shepherds Bush on the last leg of his marathon.

Right: The moment when Dorando lost his way after coming into the White City Stadium.

Facing page: The end for the gallant Italian as he collapses *(top)* and is carried off on a stretcher *(centre)*.

Moments before Dorando literally fell through the tape, the American No 1 John Joseph Hayes, who had paced himself intelligently, entered the stadium and finished with an impressive sprint and under his own steam, while at the trackside doctors were working to revive Pietri who had come close to death.

There were attempts to award the race to Dorando (he was entered in the Olympic programme as P. Dorando) but after protests from the Americans he was – inevitably under the international rules – disqualified and Hayes was quite rightly declared the Olympic champion. But it was the little candyman from Capri who had captured the hearts and imagination of the British public and Queen Alexandra was so moved by his performance that she presented him with a special gold cup, and popular song composer Irving Berlin wrote an ode in his honour. Thus Dorando became one of the immortals of Olympic history, while Hayes, a New York department store clerk, was virtually forgotten outside the United States.

Both Dorando and Hayes were hooked by the bait dangled by professional promoters and met in a re-

Above: The hero of the hour with the gold cup awarded to him by Queen Alexandra.

Top left: John Hayes is carried on a lap of honour by American team-mates after being declared the winner of the sensational 1908 Olympic marathon.

Above: Alf Shrubb, of Horsham and South London Harriers, who dominated British long-distance running at the turn of the century.

Left: Four early masters of the marathon, left to right: Alf Shrubb, Thomas Longboat, John Hayes and Pietro Dorando.

match indoors at Madison Square Garden in November 1908. They battled around 260 circuits of a wooden track, Dorando finally winning by a distance of 75 yards. Then the spindly Italian, a 5 ft 3 in bantam-weight, clashed in a 'head to head' duel with Canadian Indian Thomas Longboat and was contesting the lead when he collapsed less than a mile from the finish. Both men were paid a fee of more than £1,000 each. They met again the following month and again Dorando was forced to retire.

Professional long-distance running had become a craze in the United States and a massive crowd turned out at the New York Polo grounds to see Dorando and Hayes battle for a $10,000 prize in a race billed as 'the Marathon Derby'. Dorando saw off the challenge of Hayes but had to be content with second place behind Henri St Yves, a 5 ft tall French restaurateur who also raced to victory in the second 'Marathon Derby'.

Dorando's mentor and close friend was Alf Shrubb, the British long-distance master who was an outstanding amateur at the turn of the century until becoming a professional globetrotter who used to race against relays of runners and once, over 10 miles, against a horse when he was beaten by just 15 yards. The little Italian never forgot the warm reception he got in Britain after his gallant run in the 1908 Olympics and when he retired from running in 1912 he adopted England as his homeland. He settled in Birmingham where he ran a small cafe and was a popular character. One of his final appearances was indoors at the Royal Albert Hall where he literally ran himself dizzy on a coconut matting track on which there were no fewer than 20 laps to a mile! British professional Charlie Gardiner distinguished himself in the cramped conditions by running the marathon course in 2h 37:01·4.

When the Olympics were staged in London in 1948,

Dorando – then 64 – briefly came back into the public spotlight. He said of the 1908 marathon that had made him a legendary figure of athletics: 'I all but died in the last moments of the race. The strain was so great that my heart moved half an inch out of place and only the fact that there were doctors on hand to massage my heart saved my life.

'I have little recollection of those last few hundred yards. I just knew I had to get to the finishing line and only instinct kept me going.

'Yet amazingly I felt no ill effects once I had slept through the night and from that day to this I have not had one moment's ill health. I shall always treasure the moment when Queen Alexandra presented me with a special trophy. It meant as much to me as an Olympic gold medal.'

The world-wide publicity given to the 'Dorando Marathon' made the race one of the most popular of all sporting events and the times started to tumble as more and more athletes took up the long-distance challenge. Hayes was clocked at 2h 55:18·4 as he crossed the finishing line in the 1908 Olympics. The exhausted Pietri broke the tape in 2h 54:47·0. The following year, Britain's Fred Barrett won the first Polytechnic Harriers Windsor to Stamford Bridge marathon in 2h 42:31·0. Canadian James Corkery was first in the same event three years later in 2h 36:54·0 and was rated one of the favourites for the 1912 Olympic title in Stockholm.

Blazing heat turned Stockholm into a furnace but the Olympic officials insisted on the race being run with temperatures at their peak and 33 of the 67 competitors dropped out suffering from heat exhaustion, including Finland's talented Tatu Kolehmainen whose brother Hannes was to become the legendary 'father of long distance running'.

It was a race of tragedy for Portugal's 21-year-old Francisco Lazaro who collapsed suffering from heat stroke and later died in a Stockholm hospital. The Olympic title was won by South African champion Ken McArthur who was born in Ulster in 1883. He was running in only his second marathon but paced himself to perfection, refusing to go along with the hectic early pace. He and his South African team-mate Chris Gitsham started to move through the field in the second half of the race, finally breaking the strong challenge of American duo Gaston Strobino and Andy Sockalexis.

A victory garland was thrown over McArthur's shoulders as he turned into the Olympic stadium and he made a triumphant lap of the track before breasting through the tape in 2h 36:54·8. His compatriot Git-

Ulster-born Ken McArthur is weighed down by his victor's garland as he breaks the tape at the end of the eventful 1912 Olympic marathon in Stockholm.

sham finished second just 58 seconds later to give South Africa their greatest moment in Olympic history.

The South Africans were carried shoulder high back to their hotel by a cheering, chanting crowd and thousands of people stayed outside the South African headquarters until the early hours of the next morning as they joined in spontaneous celebrations of what had been a memorable double triumph. Few people then knew that just a 100 yards away in the Serafino Hospital poor Francisco Lazaro's life was ebbing away.

There was a jarring note to the South African victory party when Gitsham was alleged to have accused McArthur of bad sportsmanship, claiming he had broken an agreement that they should run into the stadium together. But after the story had been published it was dismissed as 'wild rumour'.

Among the 33 runners beaten by the boiling conditions was Japan's Shizo Kanakuri. When he insisted that one day he would return to finish the race, he was dismissed as an eccentric. But he kept to his word and in 1967 he returned to Stockholm and ran a final lap of the Olympic stadium. So he finished the race exactly 54 years, 8 months, 6 days, 8 hours, 32 minutes and 20·3 seconds after starting out on his marathon run!

HANNES KOLEHMAINEN

THE 'FATHER' OF THE FABULOUS FLYING FINNS

IT WAS 'HANNES THE MIGHTY' Kolehmainen who started the tradition of great Finnish middle and long distance running by winning three gold medals in the 1912 Stockholm Olympics. He took part in his first marathon race at the age of 17 in 1906 and 14 years later proved himself the finest marathon runner of the first quarter of the century with a remarkable victory in the 1920 Antwerp Olympics.

Hannes was the most famous and gifted of three athletic brothers: there was Tatu, who competed with him in the 1912 and 1920 Olympics, and William, who became a prominent professional runner. But it was Hannes (an abbreviation of Johannes) who became regarded as the 'father' of Finnish running and his exploits inspired Paavo Nurmi, perhaps the finest of all the flying Finns, to follow a career in athletics. Much later in the Finnish 'family tree' came Lasse Viren, who admits to having got his early incentive to run by listen-

'Hannes the Mighty' Kolehmainen on his way to a marathon victory in his homeland of Finland (*facing page*) and crowned with his laurel wreath (*right*) after winning the 1920 Olympic marathon.

ing to tales of the feats of Kolehmainen and Nurmi.

The Kolehmainen legend of invincibility began in Stockholm when he won the 10,000 metres, the 5,000 metres and the 8,000 metres cross-country race. His effortless, economic style was the despair of his hard-worked opponents as they watched him race easily to two Olympic records and a world record in the 3,000 metres team race (in which he received a silver medal because his team-mates were unable to give him sufficient support).

Including heats in the 1912 Games, Hannes ran a total of more than 25 miles and was the first to finish in every race that he started. Frenchman Jean Bouin, world record holder for the greatest distance run in an hour, was the only athlete to give him any real opposition but the Finn timed his home-stretch run to perfection to win a thrilling 5,000 metres race by a stride. It proved he had a steely competitive edge to go with his natural speed and stamina, a fact that he underlined in the Olympic marathon eight years later.

Kolehmainen went to live in the United States in 1913, where he won five national championships including the marathon and set a procession of new American track and road records. He returned home to Finland in time to compete for his country in the 1920 Games in Antwerp where he produced a magnificent run in the marathon.

South African Chris Gitsham, silver medallist in Stockholm, shared the lead with him up to the halfway stage but then the Finn began to pull away and seemed set for a comfortable victory. But as Kolehmainen pounded the cold and wet streets of Antwerp on his

Hannes Kolehmainen (*left*) pips French ace Jean Bouin to win the 5,000 metres in the 1912 Stockholm Olympics.

Below: Albin Stenroos, Kolehmainen's successor as Olympic marathon champion.

long and lonely way back to the Olympic stadium, Juri Lossman of Estonia started to break away from the main field that included Kolehmainen's elder brother Tatu. From having the race almost to himself, Hannes suddenly found himself under pressure.

As they turned into the stadium for one lap of the track to the finishing line, the Finn's lead had been cut to mere seconds but Kolehmainen had cleverly conserved effort for the run-in and he accelerated away to win impressively in 2h 32:35·8. This was more than 3 minutes faster than the previous world's best time for the event set by Sweden's Alex Ahlgren when winning the Windsor to Stamford Bridge marathon in 1913.

What made Kolehmainen's performance all the more stunning was that the course was later found to be 605 yards longer than the official marathon distance so he was robbed of the chance of being one of the first men inside the 2 hr 30 min-barrier. His brother William had set an unofficial world's best for the marathon when recording 2h 29:39·2 in a professional race at Newark, New Jersey, on 20 October 1912. Hannes continued running into his mid-30s, retiring after setting world records at 25,000 metres and 30,000 metres in 1922.

With the 'Untouchable' Kolehmainen retired, the United States were confident they would capture the gold medal in the 1924 Olympic marathon in Paris. They had an outstanding candidate in Clarence DeMar who had proved himself almost in the Kolehmainen class on the roads and tracks of America.

But yet another Finn emerged to conquer the world, this time 35-year-old Albin Stenroos who had collected a bronze medal behind Kolehmainen in the 10,000 metres back in 1912. He won a gruelling race through the streets of Paris in 2h 41:22·6, with Italian Romeo Bertini taking the silver medal nearly 6 minutes back in second place.

DeMar had to be content with a bronze medal but continued to build an impressive reputation on the other side of the Atlantic. He won the Boston marathon an unprecedented seven times between 1911 and 1930, his final victory coming at the age of 42. DeMar was known in the United States as 'Mr Marathon' and his long running record confounded medical experts who had advised him to quit the sport after an examination just before the 1911 Boston event revealed that he had a heart murmur.

He then went out and won the 24·7 mile race in a course record of 2h 21:39·6. Worried about his suspect

El Ouafi (*left* and *above*) who won the Olympic marathon for France in Amsterdam in 1928.

heart, he stopped racing a year later but the call of the road was too strong and he returned to marathon running in 1917. Born into a large and poor Ohio family in 1888, DeMar had been forced to quit university to support his widowed mother but not before he had been bitten by the running bug. He could never get the bug out of his system and continued running marathons until he was 66 by which time he had completed the marathon course more than 100 times.

DeMar claimed the curiosity of the medical world and he became one of the first guinea pigs of the Harvard Fatigue Laboratory where extensive tests revealed that far from having a weak heart he had astonishing cardiovascular stamina. DeMar's extraordinary consistency was matched in the 1950s by John Kelley who won eight successive USA marathon championships but – like DeMar – he was happiest on the home roads of America.

France captured a second Olympic marathon title in Amsterdam in 1928. Boughera El Ouafi, a 29-year-old Arab from Algeria, produced a sustained burst over the last 2 miles to break the challenge of five rivals and win in 2h 32:57·0.

Perhaps the most significant feature of the race was the impressive showing of competitors from Japan and South America where the marathon craze that had swept Europe and the United States had now clearly caught on. The next two Olympic gold medals would go to new territory.

SAM FERRIS

THE BRITISH MARATHON MASTER WHO BECAME 'THE NEARLY MAN' OF ROAD RUNNING

SHUFFLING SAM FERRIS was the finest of Britain's marathon runners between the two world wars but could never finish better than second in the major championship races. He showed an amazing consistency in the Polytechnic run from Windsor to Chiswick, winning the event a record eight times between 1925 and 1933.

Ferris, born in Ireland in 1900, made three bold bids for the Olympic marathon title. He finished fifth in Paris in 1924 and eighth in Amsterdam in 1928. There were indications that he had been overtaken as Britain's No 1 marathon master when Harry Payne clocked an unofficial world's best time of 2h 30:57·6 on the Windsor to Stamford Bridge route in 1929. Then Ferris was beaten into second place by Scotland's Douglas (Dunkie) Wright in the first British Empire Games in Hamilton, Ontario in 1930.

But Ferris – winner of 12 out of 19 marathons – still had his greatest marathon moment to come. Paavo Nurmi, the most famous of the flying Finns, had been the pre-race favourite for the gold medal in the 1932 Olympic marathon in Los Angeles but just prior to the opening ceremony it was announced that the undisputed king of distance running had been barred because of alleged professionalism. Nurmi was a sad spectator as he watched the tightest finish in the history of the punishing race.

Just 65 seconds covered the first four runners, with 20-year-old Argentinian student Juan Carlos Zabala beating Ferris into second place by just 100 yards which is the equivalent of an inches victory in a sprint race. Zabala won in 2h 31:26·0. Finn Armas Toivanen was third – 17 seconds behind Ferris – and Dunkie Wright finished fourth only 65 seconds adrift of the winner.

Zabala's victory was a triumph almost as much for his coach, Andrew Stirling, as for himself. Stirling, a globetrotting Scottish physical education teacher, had

Juan Carlos Zabala (*above*), left is about to break the challenge of Canadian Bricker on his way to victory in the 1932 Los Angeles Olympic marathon.

Facing page: Britain's Sam Ferris, a master of the marathon who collected a silver medal behind Zabala.

spotted Zabala's potential when he was coaching in Argentina. Zabala was just 13 and an orphan. Stirling virtually adopted him and put him on a training schedule that turned him into a world-class athlete within five years.

After he had won the South American 10,000 metres title at the age of 20, Stirling took Zabala to Europe to prepare him for the 1932 Olympics. He quickly settled to his new surroundings and set a world record for 30 km (18·64 mile) in Vienna in October 1931. Then in his marathon debut he won the challenging Kosice event.

Under pressure from Sam Ferris, Zabala ran himself to the edge of exhaustion in Los Angeles and collapsed after clinching a memorable Olympic victory.

It was a magnificent run by Ferris, yet he might have

The competitors in the 1936 Berlin Olympics start out on their marathon run (*facing page*) in the shadow of a forest of swastikas. The eventual winner Kitei Son (No 382, *above*) was always among the leaders, while 1932 Olympic champion Juan Zabala (*below*) set too fast a pace in defence of his title and cracked under pressure from Son.

done even better. While making final preparations for the race he had picked out an advertising hoarding half a mile from the stadium as a marker for when he planned to pick up pace for an all-out run to the finish. The vast crowd that lined the marathon route hid the hoarding from his sight and so he left his sprint effort too late to snatch the gold medal.

A Scot, Duncan McNab Robertson, rivalled even the formidable Ferris for consistency in home-staged marathons. Over a period of nearly 20 years from 1928 he won the AAA title six times and was once second and once third. He seemed to make a habit of getting himself involved in exciting finishes, twice winning the AAA title by just a matter of yards. One of these victories was over Ernie Harper, who gained revenge a few weeks later when he finished second in the 1936 Berlin Olympic marathon with Robertson back in seventh place.

The marathon bug had bitten deep in the Far East by the mid-1930s and in 1935 western road runners were staggered by the news that the 2 hr 30 min-barrier had been beaten in three separate races in Japan, first by Fusashige Suzuki (2h 27:49·0), then by Yasuo Ikenaka (2h 26:44·0) and finally by Kitei Son whose time of 2h 26:42·0 would last as a world's best time for more than 11 years.

Kitei Son, born in Korea but running for Japan, won the gold medal at the Berlin Olympics in 2h 29:19·2. Defending champion Juan Zabala had set off at a suicidal pace and Ernie Harper signalled to Kitei Son that they should let him go. 'I knew it would be impossible for him to continue at that sort of speed,' Harper said later when celebrating his silver medal success. Sure enough Zabala 'blew up' and dropped out of the race suffering from exhaustion. Son drew away from Harper over the last 2 miles to win by a margin of 2 min 3 sec.

Son, just 21, astonished the athletics world by announcing that he would never again run another marathon. But he had an influence on the event in later years when he coached Kee Yong Ham, the 19-year-old Korean who won the Boston marathon in 1950.

There were familiar faces battling it out on Britain's roads in the immediate post-war years. The first AAA marathon championship of peacetime saw an almost carbon copy of the 1939 race when Duncan Robertson had beaten Squire Yarrow in a close race. This time the race was even closer with the two rivals – both now 41 years old – locked together as they raced around London's White City track on the final lung-bursting 385 yards. The steeplechase was still in progress as the

Argentinian Guinez leads the field at the start of the 1948 Olympic marathon *(left)* and continues to set the pace at the 2 mile mark *(above)*. But it's his countryman Delfo Cabrera *(below)* who breaks the tape at the climax of the race in Wembley Stadium.

Facing page: Jack Holden . . . padding bare-foot to the Empire Games gold medal in Auckland in 1950.

effort to reach the tape. Gailly was overhauled first by Argentinian Delfo Cabrera and then Tom Richards who became the third successive Briton to collect an Olympic silver medal in the marathon. Richards finished just 16 seconds behind Cabrera whose winning time was 2h 34:51·6. Gailly managed to struggle to the line in third place for a hard-earned bronze medal.

Britain's brightest hope in the 1948 Olympics marathon had been Jack Holden, who a year earlier had won the first of four successive AAA marathon championships. His stunning running career had stretched from 1929 and he switched from a successful track career at the end of World War II when he was 39.

Holden, a tough, likeable character from Bilston in Staffordshire, failed to finish in the 1948 Olympics because of blister problems but he more than made up for his disappointment with an incredible sequence of runs in 1950 when, in a time span of just six months, he won five marathons including the Empire and European championship races. In the February he won the Empire title at Auckland after telling his rivals in a confident rather than cocky manner: 'Take a good look at my face now because once the race starts all you're going to see is my back.' He then provided action to go with his bold words. The Tipton Harrier took an early lead and completely dictated the pace and the race. His old blister problems started bothering him after 15 miles and so he discarded his running shoes and continued on bare feet. He had to contend with the attentions of an unfriendly Great Dane 2 miles from the finish and having escaped with nipped calves carried on to win by 4 minutes in 2h 32:57·0. 'I was just glad that the dog didn't fancy British meat,' said Holden who was himself a dog lover and a breeder of Staffordshire terriers.

Six months later, 43-year-old Holden underlined his supremacy over many of the world's best marathon runners when he won the European championship in Brussels in 2h 32:13·2. He beat the title holder Mikko Hietanen of Finland by just over half a minute with the Russian champion Fyeodosiy Vanin, with whom he had contested the lead for most of the race, finishing third. Holden's victory broke Finland's stranglehold on the European title. Finns won the championship in four of the first five marathon title races.

While Holden had proved himself the 'King of the Road' in Brussels, it was a bouncing Czech called Emil Zatopek who took the crown on the track with runaway victories in the 5,000 and 10,000 metres. Two years later he was to turn his attention to the most challenging race of them all: The Marathon.

two men battled side by side towards the tape, first one getting a chest ahead and then the other. Stragglers in the steeplechase stood to one side and became spectators of the dramatic race and joined in the applause as Yarrow, 1938 European silver medallist, hurled himself through the tape to win by a mere fifth of a second. It was the closest marathon finish on record.

The 1946 European championship in Oslo provided a sensation when the winning time for Finland's Mikko Hietanen was announced as a world's best 2h 24:55·0. But when the course was remeasured it was found to be a mile short of the official distance. There were no doubts, however, that Korean Yun Bok Suh had set new figures when he covered the tough Hopkinton to Boston course in 2h 25:39·0 on 19 April 1947.

There was almost a repeat of the 'Dorando Marathon' as a dramatic climax to the 1948 London Olympics. Belgian Etienne Gailly forced the pace for much of the race but had not broken all his rivals as he turned into Wembley Stadium for the final lap. The 21-year-old paratrooper had run himself out and could hardly put one foot in front of the other as he made a desperate

EMIL ZATOPEK

THE BOUNCING CZECH WHO TURNED EVERY RACE TO GOLD

THERE HAS NEVER BEEN another runner quite like Emil Zatopek. He ran more miles than possibly any other track athlete in history and looked as if he hated

Running was agony and ecstasy for Emil Zatopek (*facing page*) and British stars like Gordon Pirie and

Derek Ibbotson (*above*) usually had to be content with a view of his back.

every second of it. When he ran, his head lolled from side to side and his face was contorted in agony with his tongue hanging out like somebody being strangled. He bounced around the track at uneven pace, sometimes slowing to converse with other runners and then tearing off on lung-bursting spurts that sapped the strength, stamina and willpower of his rivals. The fact that his strange tactics were successful is proved by his long-running record of victories. During a great and glorious career he set 18 world records from distances of 5,000 metres to 30,000 metres.

The athletics world watched with fascination when he switched from the track to the road for his first marathon in the 1952 Olympics where he had already pocketed the gold medals for the 5,000 and 10,000 metres. He was chasing what was considered the 'impossible' treble.

Zatopek had revealed his potential to the world in the 1948 Olympics in London when he won the 10,000 metres and took the silver in the 5,000 metres after leaving an astonishing finishing burst just too late to catch Belgian Gaston Reiff. He had started the last lap 70 metres adrift of Reiff and was just a stride behind at the tape, a performance that revealed Zatopek's eccentricity and also his determination.

Born the seventh of eight brothers and sisters in Koprinice, Moravia, on 19 September 1922, Emil did not become interested in running until the age of 18 when working in a shoe factory. He was persuaded by workmates to run at a local meeting and surprised himself by finishing second. By the time he was 22 he had broken the Czech records for 2,000, 3,000 and

5,000 metres and after joining the army in 1945 he stepped up his punishing training schedule until he was running an average of 15 miles a day, often while wearing his heavy army boots.

His first major international test came in the 1946 European championships in Oslo when he finished fifth in the 5,000 metres, won by Britain's Sydney Wooderson. This experience of top competitive athletics encouraged him to train even harder and by the time of the London Olympics he had developed into one of the world's outstanding middle distance runners. But he was still four years short of his peak. That came in Helsinki in 1952.

Zatopek's 1952 gold rush started on Sunday 20 July when he lined up with 30 other runners for the 10,000 metres. He dominated the race after five laps during which he seemed almost bored by the procession.

Suddenly he unleashed a long sprint that 'killed off' most of his competitors. Only Britain's Gordon Pirie and French Algerian Alain Mimoun could present any sort of a challenge but they too were dropped when he put in a devastating last lap to clinch a convincing victory in 29 min 17·0 sec, which chopped 42·6 sec off the Olympic record he had set in London.

He was back on the track two days later for his heat of the 5,000 metres when he was content to stroll across the finish line in third place after spending much of the race chatting to his rivals. The final was far from casual, with Zatopek having to work furiously hard for his victory. With 300 metres to go, Britain's Chris Chataway was in the lead with German Herbert Schade, Mimoun and Zatopek chasing at his heels. Chataway, close to exhaustion, stumbled against the curb and sprawled on the track as Zatopek made his dash for

Emil Zatopek surges towards the tape and victory in the 5,000 metres final in the 1952 Helsinki Olympics. He is chased by Frenchman Alain Mimoun and German Herbert Schade. They have just swept past Britain's Chris Chataway, who stumbled against the curb and fell coming into the final straight.

victory. Mimoun and Schade tried to respond but could not match the Czech's finishing speed as he broke the tape in a new Olympic record of 14 min 06·6 sec.

That same afternoon Zatopek's wife, Dana, who was born on exactly the same day as Emil, won the gold medal in the javelin with an Olympic record throw of 165 ft 7 in (50·47 m).

Then on Sunday 27 July Zatopek turned his attention to the 'impossible' treble. He had never competed in a marathon before and was so unsure of what pace to set that he decided to follow the British race favourite Jim Peters. Sharing the lead at the halfway stage with Zatopek and Sweden's Gustav Jansson, Peters was

suddenly cursed by an attack of cramp and reluctantly had to drop out. Zatopek had lost his pacemaker and decided to go it alone. He produced one of the sprints that epitomised his track style and went away to win by more than 2 minutes from Argentinian Reinaldo Gorno, with Jansson taking the bronze medal. Zatopek's time was an Olympic record 2h 23:03·2.

Reflecting on this race some time later, Zatopek said: 'If you want to run, then run a mile. If you want to experience another life, run a marathon.'

He wound down his memorable Olympic career in Melbourne in 1956 when he finished sixth in the marathon, which was won by his old rival Alain Mimoun,

Emil Zatopek (*facing page*) and Alain Mimoun (*left*) are four years apart as they each start the last lap of their golden Olympic marathon runs. Zatopek (*below*) is wrapped in a blanket after finishing sixth in the Melbourne Games and congratulates his old foe Mimoun (*bottom left*) on his long-awaited victory.

who had won five silvers (three Olympic and two European) behind the great Czech.

It was a remarkable achievement by Mimoun who had been hobbling around with the aid of a stick just a year earlier with recurring pains in his feet that would have forced lesser men into retirement. But Mimoun, born Ali Mimoun O'Kacha in Algeria in 1921, was obsessed by the ambition of winning an Olympic gold medal. He finished an undistinguished twelfth in the 10,000 metres in Melbourne but insisted on going ahead with his first-ever marathon challenge. The race got off to an hilarious false start and then Mimoun, with his distinctive shuffling style, moved steadily through

the field and went on to win by 1½ minutes in exactly 2h 25.

Mimoun was something of a miracle man of running. His career seemed ended almost before it had begun during World War II. He was wounded in the left leg while fighting with the French forces in the Battle of Monte Cassino in Italy. But he claimed he was born to run and established himself as a top-flight competitor soon after the end of the war. Among his achievements were four victories in the tough International Cross Country Championship – in 1949, 1952, 1954 and 1956.

When injury threatened to force him out of the 1956 Olympics, he vowed: 'I will be there. All the omens point to a French victory in the marathon. We won it in 1900 and again in 1928. The gap is again 28 years and I would like to try to win the event for France again . . .' While making final preparations for the race in Melbourne he heard his wife had given birth to a baby.

Facing page: The remarkable Alain Mimoun wins the International Cross Country championship for a fourth time and *(inset)* receives his winner's wreath.

Alain Mimoun (No 1 *left*) leads a race through the streets of Paris and *(below)* enjoys a reunion with his old friend and rival Emil Zatopek.

'Now I am even more determined to win the race in celebration,' he said.

He was always among the leaders and he set such a brisk pace that the first six to finish were all inside the 2 hr 30 min-barrier. His gold medal took pride of place in his collection alongside the medal he had been awarded for gallantry during the war.

Mimoun shrugged aside photographers and officials after his victory to stand anxiously at the trackside waiting for the sixth man to finish. It was the man he had followed home so many times in the past, Emil Zatopek, and as he crossed the finishing line Mimoun gave his old rival and friend a welcoming hug.

It was Zatopek's last run. He returned home to Czechoslovakia where he was severely censured for publicly supporting the Dubcek government in their stand against Russian domination in 1968. He lost his Communist Party membership, his rank of colonel in the Czech army and his position of coach to the Dukla Prague athletic team. But he never lost the esteem and admiration of the followers of world sport who considered him one of the greatest athletes of all time, whose integrity, sportsmanship and sheer talent were legendary.

JIM PETERS

THE MARATHON AGONY OF THE LIONHEART OF VANCOUVER

THE 'MILE OF THE CENTURY' between Roger Bannister and John Landy had just finished in the Empire Games at Vancouver on 7 August 1954, Bannister bringing the capacity crowd to its feet with an electric finishing burst that carried him to a dramatic victory in 3 min 58·8 sec. The spectators settled down to await the finish of the marathon, while the sportswriters concentrated on polishing descriptive accounts of the Bannister-Landy duel. They were understandably convinced that this would be their best story of the day because the news from the marathon was that it had developed into literally a runaway race for Britain's Jim Peters. It was into its closing stages and Peters was 3 miles ahead of his nearest rival.

The race had started in a heat haze and the pace was too hot for most of the 16 competitors, nine of whom failed to finish the course. *The fact that one of those nine was Jim Peters provided one of the most tragic sports stories of all time.*

At the time of the Vancouver marathon, 35-year-old Peters was one of the world's most successful and experienced distance runners. The war had delayed his entry into top-flight athletics but he gave an indication of his potential when he won the AAA 6 miles title in 1946. Two years later he represented Britain in the Olympic 10,000 metres and was so depressed at being lapped by both Emil Zatopek and Alain Mimoun that he decided to retire from athletics and concentrate on his career as an optician in Essex.

Facing page: Jim Peters, the British lionheart who answered the call of the road.

But the call of the road was too strong and he made a comeback in dramatic fashion in the Polytechnic Windsor-Chiswick Marathon in 1951. He overtook the 'Old Master' Jack Holden in the closing stages to become the first Briton to win a marathon inside two and a half hours. It was the first of four astonishing victories in successive years over the Windsor-Chiswick course and on the last three occasions he lowered the world's best time for the marathon. His clockings were 2h 20:42·2 (1952), 2h 18:40·2 (1953), 2h 17:39·4 (1954).

After he and his redoubtable British rival Stan Cox had failed to make their expected impressive impact on the 1952 Olympic marathon, there were rumours that Peters would again retire. The thought never entered his head and, ignoring those who claimed his training under coach 'Johnny' Johnston was severe to the point of self destruction, he stepped up his punishing schedule to 115 miles per week. A series of victories, including in the prestigious Enschede and Turku marathons, suggested he was on the right road towards his target of a gold medal in the 1954 Empire Games.

As a warm up for the marathon, Peters competed in the Empire Games 6 miles and signalled that he was in form by collecting a bronze medal. He knew only one way to run and that was out in front as a trail blazer and that was how he decided to run the marathon on that scorching Saturday afternoon in August 1954.

Boldly – some claimed foolishly – he ignored the sweltering conditions and set a pace that 'killed off' a cluster of his rivals including Stan Cox, who was helped off the course after running into a telegraph pole. Peters

had a seemingly unassailable lead as he reached the stadium but the conditions and his suicidal pace had left him dangerously dehydrated. The steep gradient of the entrance tunnel leading into the stadium unhinged his remaining sense of balance.

He lurched on to the track like a drunken man lost in a maze. It took him 11 agonising minutes to cover just 200 of the remaining 385 yards to the tape. He fell eight times . . . he staggered . . . he crawled as a courageously determined mind and spirit tried to conquer and control an utterly exhausted body.

Nobody dared help this pitiful, white-clad figure because a touch would have meant disqualification as in Dorando's infamous Olympic marathon in London in 1908. Peters the lionheart was finally picked up from the track, a totally broken man. He was gently placed on a stretcher by giant English shot putter John Savidge and was rushed to an oxygen tent where he was fed intravenously with life-saving saline and glucose. Peters briefly regained consciousness and asked a

nurse: 'Did I win?' She gave him a reassuring smile and tactfully replied: 'You did very well.' He was then taken to hospital where he spent two days hovering between life and death before his renowned fighting spirit pulled him through.

Meanwhile the Empire Games gold medal had been won by Scotland's Joe McGhee who, despite once tripping himself, ran on to finish in 2h 39:36·0. It was wrongly reported that McGhee had been sitting in a ditch waiting for an ambulance to pick him up when he heard that Peters had failed to finish.

'This was absolute rubbish,' McGhee said later. 'I had been locked in a battle with two South Africans from the 22-miles mark and when I managed to pull away from them I thought I was on my way to second place and was delighted with my effort. It was not until I was near to the stadium that I learnt I was in first place.'

It will always be remembered as the Jim Peters race, as the 1908 Olympic marathon has gone down in history

The last agonising moments for Jim Peters in the Vancouver marathon. A shirt-sleeved Chris Brasher (second left at the track-side on the facing page) urges Peters on. John Savidge, the giant English shot putter who picked him up from the track after his final collapse, watches anxiously behind the policeman.

Right: Sergey Pop   the 1958 European champion

winning the European championship in Stockholm in 1958.

Popov, a tiny 5 ft 3 in Trans-Siberian Railway mechanic who was born in Irkutsk close to the Mongolian border in 1930, led from start to finish. Once he had cracked 1956 Olympic champion Alain Mimoun at 15 miles he never looked in any danger and finally won by a mile from his Russian team-mate Ivan Filin.

There have been few unluckier marathon men than Filin. In the 1954 European championship in Berne, he was the leader coming into the stadium but was misdirected by a track official. By the time he retraced his steps he had lost precious seconds and Finland's Veikko Karvonen and another Russian, Boris Grishayev, were ahead of him. Karvonen won in 2h 24:51·6. Filin had to be satisfied with a bronze medal, despite the Jury of Appeal conceding that he would 'have undoubtedly won' but for being pointed in the wrong direction.

Popov started the 1960 Olympic marathon in Rome as one of the favourites. He completed the course nearly 4 minutes inside the previous best time for the Olympic event yet finished in only fifth place. He had been swept aside by the emergence of a new power in marathon running – from Africa.

as the Dorando race. McGhee – like 1908 Olympic champion John Hayes – became a forgotten man of the marathon. Jim Peters, just 185 yards short of golden glory, was presented with a special medal by the Duke of Edinburgh. It was inscribed, '. . . a token of admiration for a most gallant marathon runner.' Peters never raced again.

South African Jackie Mekler was another outstanding marathon runner in the 1950s and he collected a silver medal in the Vancouver Empire Games behind McGhee. He had a best time for the 26 miles 385 yards race of 2h 27:53·4 but was even more impressive at 'ultramarathon' running. He won the famous 54-mile Comrades Marathon from Durban to Pietermaritzburg five times to equal the record shared by legendary 'old comrades' Wally Hayward, Arthur Newton and Hardy Ballington.

The Jim Peters world's best time of 2h 17:39·4 survived for four years before Russian Sergey Popov lowered it by more than 2 minutes to 2h 15:17·0 when

ABEBE BIKILA

THE BARE-FOOT EMPEROR'S GUARD WHO LED THE BLACK AFRICAN ATHLETICS EXPLOSION

ABEBE BIKILA, a member of Emperor Haile Selassie's Imperial Bodyguard in Ethiopia, brought black Africa its first Olympic gold medal in athletics when he padded bare-foot through the streets of Rome to win the 1960 marathon in a world-best time of 2h 15:16·2. It was an astonishing victory that heralded the start of the emerging power of Africans in the world of athletics and there was further proof of the talent waiting to be tapped when Moroccan Rhadi Ben Abdesselem finished second just 200 yards behind Bikila.

It was somehow ironic and fitting that Bikila should choose Rome as the stage for his magnificent run. He had been just 3 years old when his country had been invaded by Mussolini's Italian troops. Now it was his

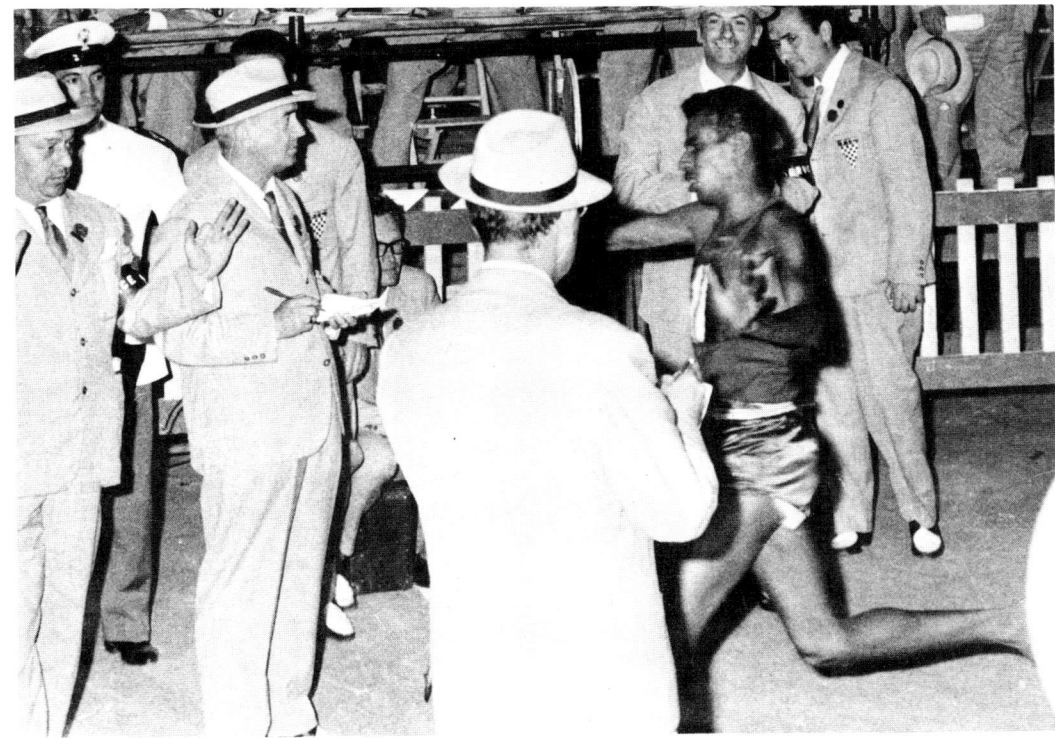

Abebe Bikila pads to victory in the 1960 Olympic marathon in Rome and (*facing page*) celebrates his triumph as his team-mates give him a winning lift.

BIKILA

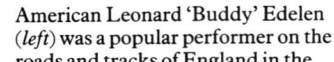

American Leonard 'Buddy' Edelen (*left*) was a popular performer on the roads and tracks of England in the 1960s and he was often the trail blazer as in this 10 miles race at Hurlingham in 1963 (*below*).

turn to conquer and thousands of Italian spectators lined the moonlit route to sportingly cheer on the Ethiopian as he glided smoothly across the cobbled streets of the historic Appian Way, his economical stride unhindered by the uneven surface that caused blistering problems for many of his well-shod rivals.

This was the first Olympic marathon lit by the moon. The organisers wisely decided on a near-dusk start to save the runners from competing in the potentially killing heat of the afternoon sun. It was clear from the halfway mark that the race for the gold medal was between Bikila and Moroccan cross-country star Rhadi, with New Zealander Barry Magee coming through strongly over the second half of the course to take the bronze medal.

As Bikila and Rhadi battled along the Appian Way (Via Appia, the 'Queen of the Roads' built in 312 BC), Italian soldiers lit the way with flaming torches. Bikila, trained to a pitch of perfection by Scandinavian coach Onni Niskanen, finally broke Rhadi's spirited challenge just a kilometre from home and he had stretched his winning lead to 25 seconds as he broke the tape under the Triumphal Arch of Constantine at the foot of the Capitol Hill.

The modest, 5 ft 10 in tall Ethiopian, who had not bothered to take a single drink during his run, commented afterwards that the only time he was in any trouble was when an enthusiastic spectator on a motor scooter had veered dangerously close to him. 'Other than that,' said Bikila, 'it was a very comfortable run.'

It was the start of an explosion of black African talent. All the signs were there in the Rome marathon, with four of the first eight places being filled by 'unknown' African runners.

A major talking point before the 1964 Games in Tokyo was whether Bikila could become the first marathon champion to win the Olympic title for a second time. The competition was going to be tougher than ever before. In the gap between the two Olympic championships, the world's best marathon time had been trimmed three times. Japanese Toru Terasawa clocked 2h 15:15·8 at Beppu in February 1963. Four months later American Leonard Edelen chopped it to 2h 14:28·0 when winning the Windsor-Chiswick marathon. In the same event the following year, Britain's Basil Heatley produced a storming run to win in 2h 13:55·0.

Basil Heatley (504 *above*) built up reserves of stamina and strength on the cross-country circuit that helped him to victory in the 1964 Windsor to Chiswick marathon (*below*) and a silver medal in the Tokyo Olympics.

Two views of Abebe Bikila breaking the tape *(left and below)* in the 1964 Tokyo Games to retain his Olympic crown – a magnificent performance whichever way you look at it!

It was Heatley who was installed as the Olympic favourite after it was learned that Bikila was to have his appendix removed just five weeks before the Games in Tokyo. But the Ethiopian was no ordinary human being and his powers of recovery were such that he was in peak condition for the defence of his title. Australian track star Ron Clarke set a cracking pace but after an hour it was obvious that Bikila was again going to emerge triumphant as first of all he broke the challenge of Clarke and then Ireland's bold Jim Hogan (who touched his peak form two years later when winning the European championship).

Bikila was 4 minutes ahead of the field as he went

through the tape in another new world's best time of 2h 12:11·2. This time he wore running shoes and he cut an almost comical figure in his green vest and scarlet shorts as he dropped on to his back in the centre of the stadium and started a rapid sequence of bicycling exercises while waiting for his rivals to finish the race.

The race for the silver medal developed into a drama-tic two-man struggle between Basil Heatley and Japa-nese Kokichi Tsuburaya who entered the stadium first just seconds ahead of the fast-finishing Briton and obviously in distress. He could not respond when Heatley drew level with just 200 metres to go and for the fourth time in an Olympic marathon the silver medal went to a British runner. Poor Tsuburaya felt so humi-

liated at being overtaken so close to the finishing line in front of his fanatical supporters that he went into a deep depression and some months later committed hara-kiri.

Brian Kilby gave a further boost to British marathon running by finishing fourth after making a late break away from Hungarian Jozsef Suto and American ace Leonard 'Buddy' Edelen, who was a well-known and popular performer on the British long-running circuit. Kilby, a stalwart member of the Coventry Godiva Harriers, was an impressive winner of five successive AAA marathon titles and touched the peak of his distinguished career in 1962 when winning both the European and Commonwealth Games titles. His fastest run over the distance was 2h 14:43·0 when winning the Welsh open title at Port Talbot in July 1963.

But Kilby, like all the world's top marathon masters, had to learn to live in the shadow of Bikila who attempted to pull off a hat-trick of Olympic marathon victories in the 1968 race in Mexico. However, a leg injury forced him out of the race after 17 kilometres and it was won by his compatriot Mamo Wolde, who had earlier won a silver medal in the 10,000 metres.

Britain was powerfully represented in the 1968 Olympic marathon by Bill Adcocks, Tim Johnston and 1966 Commonwealth Games champion Jim Alder. They were unlucky to be at their peak in the year the Games marathon was run at altitude.

Adcocks had been in magnificent form leading up to the Olympics. He returned a British-best time of 2h 12:16·8 in the Karl Marx Stadt event in May 1968. This clipped more than a minute off the previous best time recorded by Scot Alastair Wood in a run from Inverness to Forres in July 1966. Adcocks was the first of the British trio to finish in Mexico, coming home in a creditable fifth place in 2h 25:33·0. Two months later the Coventry Godiva Harrier lowered his British best 'record' to 2h 10:47·8 when competing in the tough Fukuoka marathon in Japan.

Tim Johnston, who had devoted a year of his life training at altitude in preparation for the Mexico Games, was handicapped by stomach cramps and performed wonders to finish in eighth place in 2h 28:04·0. Jim Alder was hardest hit by the altitude and the crazy decision to run the race in the full heat of the afternoon and was so dehydrated at 30 kilometres that he lost his sense of balance. It was at that stage of the race that the smooth-moving Wolde picked up the pace of the race and pulled away to win by over 3 minutes from Kenji Kimihara of Japan and New Zealander Mike Ryan. Wolde's winning time was 2h 20:26·4, more than 8 minutes outside the Olympic record set by his country-

Facing page: Brian Kilby, European and Commonwealth marathon master in 1962.

Mamo Wolde keeps the Olympic marathon title for Ethiopia in the 1968 Games in Mexico *(left)* and is on his way to a silver medal in the 10,000 metres *(below)*, with Ron Clarke (102) and Ron Hill (404) among the chasing pack.

man Abebe Bikila in Tokyo four years earlier.

There is, sadly, a tragic sequel to the remarkable Abebe Bikila story. He was severely injured in a car crash and was confined to a wheelchair following treatment at the famous Stoke Mandeville paraplegic hospital in England. A resilient and cheerful character, he refused to let his injury curtail his life as a competitive sportsman and he became a keen exponent of paraplegic sports, particularly archery.

Abebe Bikila died following a brain haemorrhage in October 1973. He was 41. He will always live on in Olympic legend as one of *the* Kings of the Marathon.

DEREK CLAYTON

THE BRITISH-BORN AUSTRALIAN WHO DEFIED DOCTORS TO BECOME THE MARATHON MIRACLE MAN

DOCTORS SADLY SHOOK THEIR HEADS when they examined the extent of Derek Clayton's Achilles tendon injury in 1967. The tendon was shattered and the 24-year-old Clayton was told that his promising running career was almost certainly at an end. He had taken up marathon running two years earlier and looked to have tremendous potential. But as he hobbled around on crutches after a long and delicate operation, there seemed no way he could return to the road.

Clayton's first target after the operation was to start walking again. Then he started jogging. Relieved to find there were no ill effects, he began a gentle running programme and within six months of the operation was back on a marathon training schedule. In December 1967, less than a year after being told his running days were virtually over, Clayton became the first to break the 2 hr 10 min-barrier.

Competing in the Fukuoka marathon in Japan on 3 December 1967, he won in an astounding 2h 09:36·4. This slashed nearly two and a half minutes off the previous world's best time set by Japan's Morio Shigematsu on the Windsor-Chiswick run on 12 June 1965.

Clayton had become not only the world's fastest marathon runner but also the first to complete the endurance course at an average speed of less than 5 minutes per mile. Born in Barrow-in-Furness, Lancashire, in 1942, Clayton had moved with his family to Belfast when he was 8 and emigrated with them to Australia in 1963. It was there that he started giving total concentration to athletics and it was when he stepped up from track running to the road that he began to carve an international reputation.

At 6 ft 2 in and 160 lb, Clayton dwarfed most of his marathon rivals and his 1967 Fukuoka run proved that he was big in talent as well as physique. Cartilage problems destroyed his chances of making a realistic challenge for the Olympic title in Mexico in 1968 when he did well to finish a plucky seventh.

Again he had to begin his training programme from a walking start and again he refused to be written off as finished. He increased his weekly output to 200 miles a week and stunned the athletics world again on 30 May 1969 when winning the Antwerp marathon in a mind-blowing 2h 08:33·6. He talked confidently of the possibility of breaking 2 hours for the marathon but recurring injury problems prevented him providing the action to go with his words. He failed to finish in the 1970 and 1974 Commonwealth Games and he was a well-beaten thirteenth in the 1972 Olympic Games. Disappointed that he had been unable to produce his best form at championship level, Clayton 'The Miracle Man' had the considerable consolation of knowing he would always be remembered as the first man to break the formidable 2 hr 10 min-barrier.

Ron Hill, a research textile chemist from Romiley, Cheshire, rivalled Derek Clayton for the unofficial title of world's No 1 marathon man as the 1960s gave way to the new decade of the 1970s. He was the AAA 10 miles champion five times and held world records at 10 miles, 15 miles and 25,000 metres. There were, however, question marks about his competitive qualities in the major championships. He failed to finish in the 1962

Facing page: Derek Clayton, the first man to complete the marathon course at an average speed of less than five minutes a mile.

Ron Hill (No 289 *above*) follows Belgian ace Gaston Roelants on the marathon trail in Munich.

European marathon, was way below his best in the 1964 Olympic 10,000 metres and marathon; and in 1966 he finished fifth in the Commonwealth Games 6 miles event and a disappointing twelfth in the European marathon.

He raced to a creditable seventh in the 10,000 metres in the 1968 Mexico Olympics, the first man home who did not live or train at high altitude in the build-up to the Games. But it was not until the 1969 European championship marathon that Hill at last showed that he was truly a world-class competitor. He ran the historic Marathon course at Athens with thoroughbred timing to overtake Belgian Gaston Roelants half a mile from the finish to win comfortably in 2h 16:47·8.

A few months later, despite interruption to his tough training programme, he accepted an invitation to run in the Fukuoka marathon and came in an impressive second. Then in April 1970 Hill established himself as one of the undisputed kings of the road when he became the first Briton to win the renowned Boston marathon.

His time of 2h 10:30·0 made him second only to Clayton over the marathon route.

Competing for England in the Commonwealth Games in Edinburgh on 23 July 1970, he dominated the race after 10 miles and went away to win in 2h 09:28·0, the fastest time ever recorded under championship conditions.

Hill, who lost more than half a stone from his slender 9-stone frame on the way to his memorable victory, said afterwards: 'I didn't feel all that good after four miles and wondered whether I would last the course. I was sluggish and feeling tired. But suddenly everything started to click and from halfway I was confident I was going to win. It was tough on the second half of the course because it got a lot hotter. I would have welcomed some rain but was absolutely delighted with my time. It's made all the hard work worthwhile. Now I'd like to get an Olympic medal.'

But the 1972 Munich Olympic marathon belonged to an American returning to the land of his birth.

Ron Hill flies the flag for Britain on his way to an AAA title victory. The remarkable Hill ran 67 top-class marathons.

FRANK SHORTER

THE AMERICAN ACE WHO LAUNCHED TEN THOUSAND TRIPS

FRANK SHORTER WOKE a sleeping giant when he won the marathon in the 1972 Olympics in Munich, the city where he was born to American parents in 1947. His success inspired thousands of Americans to try the marathon trip and he more than anybody was responsible for triggering the running and jogging craze that swept the United States in the 1970s.

Shorter first revealed his potential as an outstanding marathon runner when he finished second behind the formidable Kenny Moore in the 1971 AAU championship. He won the Pan-American Games marathon and the 10,000 metres later in the season and then crowned a memorable year by winning the Japanese open marathon in 2h 12:50·4.

This was just a prelude to even more impressive successes in 1972. He and Moore – a respected sportswriter – tied for first place in the US Olympic trials and he then won the Olympic title in 2h 12:19·8, this after

Frank Shorter (No 1014, *right*) is in second place on the track in the 1972 Munich Olympics but is out on his own (*facing page*) when it really matters in the closing stages of the marathon.

Frank Shorter leads the pack in Munich (*left*) and is on the trail of Cierpinski in Montreal (*below*).

setting an American record of 27 min 51·4 sec when finishing fifth in the Olympic 10,000 metres final. Shorter, by then a national idol in the United States, returned to Japan in December and won the Fukuoka marathon in a new personal best time of 2h 10:30·0, the best of his four victories in this prestigious event.

His magnificent triumph in the Munich Olympic marathon had a strange parallel with the 1904 Games in St Louis when hoaxer Fred Lorz jogged into the stadium pretending to be the marathon winner after thumbing a lift. This time Norbert Studhaus, a 22-year-old West German student, joined the race half a mile from the finish and ran fresh and strong into the Munich stadium to steal the cheers of the capacity 80,000 crowd.

As puzzled television and radio commentators tried to identify the athlete wearing a number 72 on his blue vest, officials realised that there was a joker on the track and police were called to remove him from the stadium. 'The Olympic Games have become too serious and this is my protest against the solemnity of it all,' Studhaus managed to tell reporters before being hustled away just as Frank Shorter was making his triumphant entry for a final lap of the Olympic stadium.

He completely destroyed a top-class field, breaking joint favourites Ron Hill (sixth) and Derek Clayton (thirteenth) and then going away to win by more than 2 minutes from frail-looking Belgian Karel Lismont who had won the 1971 European championship in Helsinki.

Marvellous Mamo Wolde, the winner in the 1968 Olympics in Mexico, managed to hold off American Kenny Moore for third place. Wolde, according to the record books, was 38 but it was rumoured that he was more likely over 40. His Olympic career had started in a 1,500 metres heat in Melbourne 16 years earlier.

For Frank Shorter, success could not have come at a more opportune time. By American standards, it had been a poor Olympics for their athletes and so his achievement got greater exposure than usual. His victory run was given saturation coverage on coast-to-coast television and he suddenly became a PR delight as subsequent commercial contracts proved. There had been the beginnings of a running boom in the United States shortly before the Munich Olympics but it was Shorter's magical marathon that brought thousands of Americans to their feet and out on to the roads. Health was suddenly the name of the game for people who had not bothered to move above walking speed in years. For master marathoners like Shorter and his American team-mate Bill Rodgers it also meant wealth. Sponsors saw the running and jogging boom as a shop window and it was on athletes like Shorter and Rodgers that they hung their wares.

But it was the glint of a second Olympic gold medal that took Shorter's attention in 1976 and he started favourite to retain his title, after being forced to run a gruelling marathon trial by the US Olympic selection committee just five weeks before the Games in Montreal. He beat his No 1 rival Bill Rodgers by just 7 seconds, finishing in 2h 11:51·0.

British hopes of at last finding an Olympic marathon champion had risen in 1973 when Ian Thompson made a sensational entry into the road-running ranks. Born in Birkenhead in 1949, he had been just an average club athlete with Luton United until making his marathon debut in the AAA championship on 27 October 1973 – 11 days after his twenty-fourth birthday. He had never raced more than 10 miles on the road before and most people thought he was being too ambitious when he set himself a target of 2 hr 20 min for his first marathon. Thompson astonished himself and the athletics world by winning in 2h 12:40·0, then the fastest first marathon trip of all time.

The victory earned him a place in the Commonwealth Games team and he proved he was no one-race wonder by winning the championship in Christchurch in 2h 09:12·0. He then won a major race in Athens (2h 13:50·0) and captured the 1974 European championship in 2h 13:19·0. In less than a year he had risen from novice to the world's No 1 marathoner.

Thompson, 5 ft 6½ in tall and scaling 9 st 6 lb, gave a remarkable insight into marathon running in a *Sunday Times* interview shortly before his triumph in the 1974 European championships in Rome. He said: 'For a marathon runner, I've got rather stubby legs, short levers which stand the pounding. My knees get sore, but Derek Clayton, the only man to have run a marathon faster than me, had five knee operations. It would be wrong to emphasise the pain. Pain is anaesthetised by the euphoria of running. You're going to get blisters but you stop paying attention and so they stop handing out signals. There's a part in every marathon where you lose a sense of identity in yourself. You become *running* itself.

'I've always trained hard. At 17 I was running 70 miles a week; now it's 100 and by the time of the European championships in Rome it will be 140 miles. I'm a trainee teacher, which means I can find the time.

'I have a light breakfast, two boiled eggs, bread and butter, tea without sugar. After a mid-morning coffee with sugar I go for a five-mile run in the open countryside. Then I have a stodgy school lunch, like cheese-and-egg-flan, salad, potatoes, semolina. In the evening, I run 10 miles and then eat almost anything. Today it was a chop, potatoes, oh, and semolina again.

'The marathon is 26 miles 385 yards, and the important factor is to store energy sugars – glycogen. You can only store 1,500 calories worth, which is the amount you'd burn in 1½-hours of running. My best time is

Frank Shorter where he likes to be – out in front.

just over two hours nine minutes, so you not only use up physical reserves but burn into actual muscle.

'I race on the high-carbohydrate diet. It's still controversial. You can make yourself liable to infections. Six days before the race you cut out carbohydrates, eat only protein, and continue to train at high intensity. You exhaust the body's reserves of glycogen, especially in the leg muscles. Three days before the race you switch to carbohydrates and light training. You feel good, sleep well. The glycogen increases to a much higher level than normal and enables you to go on running when everyone else is dying.

'Before my Christchurch marathon I felt so calm, I *knew* I was going to win. I'd been running ten years and felt Master of Myself. Afterwards, my legs were leaden for four or five weeks.'

After his impressive victory in the 1974 European championships in Rome, Thompson decided to prepare himself for the Montreal Olympics and so ran only one marathon in 1975 which he won in a modest 2h 24:30·0. His Olympic dream turned into a nightmare when, handicapped by an attack of cramp, he could finish only seventh in an Olympic trial race. This

was at Rotherham on 8 May 1976, a race won by 32-year-old schoolteacher Barry Watson in 2h 15:08·0 – 6 minutes outside Thompson's best time for the distance.

The British team selectors surprisingly decided to ignore Thompson's previous form and left him out of the squad when it was obvious that he had the proven class to match the world's best marathon masters. Significantly, Thompson showed a return to form four months after the Olympics when he clocked 2h 12:54·0 to finish second in the Fukuoka marathon classic in Japan. He was just 19 seconds behind Canadian winner Jerome Drayton and more than 2 minutes ahead of third man Waldemar Cierpinski, the East German who collected the gold medal in Montreal.

Ian Thompson the British king of the road whose Olympic dream turned into a nightmare.

WALDEMAR CIERPINSKI

THE 'UNKNOWN MAN' OF THE MARATHON WHO WON TWO OLYMPIC GOLD MEDALS

THE TELEVISION COMMENTATORS had no doubt that the eventual winner of the 1976 Olympic marathon was in the leading bunch after 15 miles of the Montreal endurance event. Defending champion Frank Shorter was setting the pace. With him was his American teammate Bill Rodgers, winner of the 1975 Boston marathon. At their heels were Canadian Jerome Drayton, the 1975 Fukuoka victor, and 1972 Olympic silver medallist Karel Lismont. All were thoroughbred marathoners and also there looking full of running was the latest and perhaps the greatest of the flying Finns, Lasse Viren, who was making his first marathon trip after completing the golden double of the 5,000 and 10,000 metres for the second successive Olympics.

There was a sixth man in the cluster of runners that had broken away from the rest of the field. The com-

Facing page: Waldemar Cierpinski, the double Olympic champion who will be bidding for a hat-trick of gold medals in Los Angeles in 1984.

Left: Lasse Viren, the latest and perhaps greatest of the flying Finns.

Waldemar Cierpinski (*left, below* and *facing page*) on the last lap of his golden run in the 1976 Montreal Olympics.

mentators barely mentioned him because his past record suggested he was out of his depth in such high-quality company. His name was Waldemar Cierpinski, an East German who in previous years had proved himself close to world class as a steeplechaser. But his marathon experience was so limited that nobody gave him a chance of striking gold in Montreal.

Born in Neugattersleben on 3 August 1950, he elected to step up to marathon running in 1974 for what was a basically simple reason: 'I love running and the marathon gives you the chance to do more of it than any other race.' He finished third in his marathon debut in 2h 20:28·0, a fast time considering appalling weather conditions that made every step a challenge. A year later in the same race in Kosice he improved by 3 minutes but his seventh place provided no evidence that here was a world-beater in the making. His coach Walter Schmidt stepped up his training schedule and Cierpinski proved that the extra mileage was paying dividends when he clocked 2h 13:58·0 while achieving

Waldemar Cierpinski gives a victory salute for the photographers (*top*) and takes his place on the winners' rostrum with silver medallist Frank Shorter and Karel Lismont.

his first marathon victory in the Karl Marx Stadt event in 1976. Then, competing in the East German Olympic trials, he finished such a commanding winner in 2h 12:22·0 that the selectors decided to make him a lone entrant for the Montreal marathon.

Proof of the thoroughness of the East German approach to athletics is that Cierpinski was installed in the Olympic village a full month before any of his rivals and he was encouraged to live as normally as possible so that by the time the action started he was thoroughly at home and acclimatised.

Frank Shorter admitted he had not considered Cierpinski any kind of a threat before the Montreal marathon started. 'I didn't give the guy a second thought,' he said. 'He was the only one in our leading bunch I had never seen before and I wondered who he was. He was moving impressively enough to make me realise he was going to take some watching.

'I felt I had them all beat except this one guy. I didn't even know his name or his country. He wasn't wearing the usual blue East German vest but an all-white strip and I got it into my head that he had to be Carlos Lopes of Portugal.

'When I started to put the pressure on in the last third of the race they all fell back with the exception of this unknown runner. I knew I had a battle on my hands.'

Shorter opened a 30-yard gap at one stage but Cierpinski hauled him back and was more than half a minute in the lead as he reached the stadium, crossing the finishing line in an Olympic record 2h 09:55·0. Cierpinski, looking remarkably fresh, completed another lap and ran alongside Shorter as the American finished in second place. 'We shook hands and only then did I realise he wasn't Carlos Lopes after all,' Shorter said later. 'He asked, "*Sprechen sie Deutsch?*" and I thought to myself, "That's a funny thing for a Portuguese guy to say." When I was told who he was I couldn't believe I'd been beaten by a steeplechaser!'

Shorter's time was a near personal best 2h 10:45·8, with Karel Lismont – second behind Shorter in Munich – taking the bronze medal in 2h 11:12·6. American third string Don Kardong worked his way patiently through the field to finish fourth in 2h 11:15·8, 1 min 55 sec ahead of Lasse Viren who had made such a bold bid to repeat Emil Zatopek's remarkable 1952 gold medal hat-trick.

There was talk that Cierpinski's victory had been a one-off fluke, cutting comments that were fueled by a procession of indifferent performances. In the 1978 European championship he was a well-beaten fourth and the following year he ranked only third in the East German national ratings. In December 1979 he made a third successive bid to win the classic Japanese open title at Fukuoka. Japanese runners scored a clean sweep, with Toshihiko Seko winning in 2h 10:21·0 from Hideki Kita (2h 11:05·0) and Shigera Sou (2h 11:41·0). Britain's Trevor Wright was fourth in a personal best of 2h 12:32·0, followed by European champion Leonid Moseyev of Russia (2h 12:44·0) and American Bill Rodgers (2h 12:51·0). Cierpinski, who had never managed better than third in the event, trailed in a disappointing thirty-second in a modest 2h 22:49·0. He looked a shadow of the man who had won the Montreal Olympic gold medal in such impressive style.

What the world was to discover was that Cierpinski – like Lasse Viren and Abebe Bikila before him – was a man for whom the Olympics provided the main motivation. While the 'experts' wrote him off he quietly got himself into peak mental and physical condition for his defence of the Olympic title in Moscow in 1980.

Waldemar Cierpinski, the man for whom the Olympics provide the main motivation.

Gerard Nijboer, the Flying Dutchman (*above and facing page*) who won the 1982 European marathon championship after an injury scare.

With the crack Americans and Japanese boycotting the Games, Cierpinski figured among the favourites but he was expected to encounter tough opposition from Britain's Ian Thompson, Belgian Karel Lismont, Finland's now legendary Lasse Viren, Dutchman Gerard Nijboer and the tough Russian trio Setymkul Dzhumanazarov, Vladimir Kotov and the vastly experienced Moseyev who was said to have been running up to 200 miles a week in preparation for the race.

After 25 kilometres of the Moscow marathon, Mexican track runner Rodolfo Gomez was threatening to provide one of the biggest upsets of the Games. He was quickly pulling away from a leading group that included Nijboer, the three Russians and the poker-faced Cierpinski. By 30 kilometres, the moustachioed Mexican had opened the gap to 23 seconds and his sizzling pace had already proved too much for British challengers Ian Thompson (heavy cold), David Black (shoe problems) and Bernie Ford (made dizzy by the heat) and all three had abandoned the chase. Then after an hour and a half's running Cierpinski, the man they had all been dismissing as a one race wonder, started to make his victory bid. Moving smoothly along on his mechanical, light and easy stride, he gradually brought Gomez into his sights and then picked up the pace on his run for home and a second gold medal.

Cierpinski, who was just two days short of his thirtieth birthday, came into the Moscow stadium looking as fresh and strong as when finishing triumphant in the rain of Montreal four years earlier. His time was 2h 11:03·0, good enough to put him on a privileged peak with Abebe Bikila as the only men to have won two successive Olympic marathon titles. The next four runners were inside the stadium as the East German crossed the finishing line. Nijboer, the tall, 24-year-old microbiology student, finished second just 80 metres behind to collect Holland's first Olympic athletics medal for 12 years and to confirm his early-season form when he clocked 2h 09:01·0. The Russian trio ran a typical team race but they had to settle for third, fourth and fifth places after failing to crack Cierpinski and Nijboer.

The Dutchman's career was threatened by a recurring knee injury but it was cured by acupuncture and in his next marathon run in Athens in 1982 he won the European championship in 2h 15:17·0, with Belgians Armand Parmentier and Karel Lismont second and third and a weary looking Cierpinski trailing in sixth place.

It was unfairly suggested that Cierpinski would not have won in Moscow but for the boycott by America and Japan, particularly after he had finished fifth behind four Japanese in the Fukuoka marathon just four months after his second Olympic victory. But he firmly put his critics in their place with the crushing comment: 'Like Lasse Viren, I train exclusively for the ultimate – the Olympic gold medal. All other races are merely steps along the way in my preparation.'

His dream is of an historic hat-trick of marathon victories in the 1984 Olympics in Los Angeles. Anybody who witnessed his golden runs in Montreal and then Moscow would think twice before betting against him.

Alberto Salazar, king of the New York roads.

ALBERTO SALAZAR

THE MAN FROM HAVANA WHO BECAME THE KING OF THE NEW YORK ROADS

WHEN ALBERTO SALAZAR predicted that he would complete his first marathon course in 'around 2:10 or 2:11' there were raised eyebrows among the statistically minded who realised that it was the equivalent of a miler saying he would smash 4 minutes at his first attempt at the distance. Even though he was a respected track athlete with a string of top-quality 10,000-metre runs behind him, it was generally considered that he was being more than a little ambitious with his forecast, particularly as he had never competed beyond 10 miles.

Salazar selected the bumper 1980 New York City marathon for his debut. 'I feel I am ideally suited to the marathon,' he told reporters pressing him for facts to back his bold prediction. 'My sort of shuffling style of running is economic and the distance doesn't bother me because I've always believed in piling in lots of miles in training.'

He was not being big headed; just honest. As a born-again Christian, he believed that any question asked deserved a truthful answer. 'I am entering this race to try to win it,' he said. 'I want to beat Billy Rodgers at his own game.'

Rodgers was Salazar's Greater Boston Track Club team-mate and one of the finest distance runners ever to set foot on the road. He had won the Boston marathon four times, the New York marathon four times and in the 1977-78 season became the only man to win the New York, Fukuoka and Boston marathons in succession. Nicknamed 'Boston Billy', he was described in his running-mad home town as 'the greatest runner in the history of the world'. He was certainly the wealthiest. He turned his teacher's mind to working out how he could best benefit from his running talent and became almost a one-man industry, with a chain of sports goods shops bearing his name, a magazine column, an exclusive line of running gear, special clinics and he was in demand as an after-dinner speaker and as 'a good image man' for sponsors and advertisers. There was criticism of the way Rodgers had cashed in on his fame but nobody could deny his abiity as a master marathoner. He has run more than 20 marathons faster than 2h 20 and his training schedule has been up as high as 170 miles a week. This then was the great Billy Rodgers who Salazar was talking of beating 'at his own game'.

Salazar then put action where his mouth was. He won his first ever marathon in an astounding 2h 09:41·0, the fastest debut of all time and even quicker than he had predicted. Bill Rodgers could not keep up with him and finally finished fifth, well beaten at his own game. 'Given the right conditions, I can run it faster,' said Salazar. Nobody doubted him.

Born in Havana, Cuba, on 7 August 1958, Salazar was brought to the United States at the age of 2 by his father, a former friend and supporter of Fidel Castro who didn't like the disciplines of life under communism. They lived first in Florida, then Connecticut and finally settled down at Wayland, Mass, where Alberto began to build a reputation as an outstanding schools athlete.

He progressed to an international class middle-distance runner at the University of Oregon where he came under the considerable influence of coach Bill Dellinger, a bronze medallist in the 1964 Tokyo

SALAZAR

It's impossible to spot individuals as the race gets under way (*left*) but Alberto Salazar stood out in the crowd when he crossed the finishing line (*above*) as winner of the 1982 Boston classic.
Facing page: Alberto first again, this time in the 1981 New York marathon in a world's best 2h 08·13.

Olympic 5,000 metres final. Alberto stepped up his running as an enthusiastic member of the Athletics West Club in Eugene, Oregon, and coach Dellinger commented: 'The hardest thing to do with Al is to *stop* him running. He thinks nothing of putting in around 140 to 150 miles a week and I sometimes have to put the brake on him.'

Salazar set his sights on winning the New York marathon for a second successive year and when asked to predict his time he came up with the startling reply: 'I think I can complete the course in two hours eight minutes.'

The significance of that remark was not lost on marathon fans. Salazar had committed himself to setting a new world's best time for the event in what would be only his second competitive outing over the distance.

Marathoners come in all shapes and sizes and Salazar – at 6 ft and 143 lb – is considered to have the ideal weight distribution. Scientists who have made a study of marathon running are agreed that those who carry 2 lb for every inch of height are best suited for long distance events. Alberto Salazar fits this identikit picture perfectly.

He started thorough preparations for the October 1981 New York race 17 weeks before the event and did

not miss a single day's training. To beat Derek Clayton's 12-year-old marathon 'record' Salazar knew that he had to average 4 min 54 sec for every mile.

In the early stages of the race, Irishman Louis Kenny threatened to run away with it as he set a pace that would have taken him well inside the world's best time if he had been able to maintain it. Salazar, a master at setting and holding a precision pace, did not panic as Kenny tried to break away. Finally, the Irishman ran out of steam and Salazar continued on his well-planned way and crossed the finishing line in a new world's best of 2h 08:13·0 – just 13 seconds outside his predicted time.

When he had regained his breath, Salazar commented: 'I think I can go two or three minutes faster. A time of two hours five minutes is a distinct possibility.' Alberto had spoken and nobody was arguing. A year later Alberto was back pounding the streets of New York as he made a bid to complete a hat-trick of victories in one of the world's great marathon races. He said before the start: 'I have got myself into peak condition and feel I can beat my time of last year if I'm pressed.'

There was a field of 14,307 starters for the long trek through the five boroughs of New York. Strong head-

The camera captures the colour and carnival atmosphere of the 1982 New York marathon, with Alberto Salazar (No 1) again showing the way home.

winds in the first quarter of the race wrecked any chances of a world's best time but Salazar was again the pace-setter with Mexican Rodolfo Gomez, Portuguese Carlos Lopes, American Dan Schlesinger and US-based Briton Dave Murphy keeping him company.

Salazar had run himself into a state of semi-consciousness when forcing himself across the finishing line in Boston six months earlier and there was conjecture that the experience would give him psychological problems in the later stages of the New York race. But he was in peak mental as well as physical shape and he moved majestically over the final mile to break the brave challenge of Gomez who had made such an impressive impact in the 1980 Olympic marathon in Moscow. Salazar's winning time was 2h 09:29·0, an exceptional performance considering the difficult conditions over the first seven miles. The gallant Gomez finished just 4 seconds behind in second place. Schlesinger was third in 2h 11:54·0. Murphy, making his marathon debut, was a creditable fifth in 2h 12:48·0.

'I knew I had to keep the pressure on over the last mile,' Salazar said later. 'Gomez has a faster finish than me and I was aware that I needed to weaken him. I managed to run the finish out of him but it was touch and go. He gave me a really tough race.'

With Salazar in such devastating form, it is understandable that the Americans believe they will see a home-produced marathon winner in the 1984 Olympics in Los Angeles. But the greatest event in the marathon calendar is certain to draw the cream of the world's endurance men and there are several on the horizon who look capable of giving even Salazar a run for his money.

The challengers are likely to include Australian Robert de Castella who clocked the second fastest time on record when winning the 1981 Fukuoka marathon in 2h 08:15·0, just 3 seconds outside Salazar's New York run.

ROBERT DE CASTELLA

THE AUSTRALIAN WHO TOOK A BREAKFAST-TIME RUN TO A COMMONWEALTH GOLD MEDAL

Robert de Castella, a 25-year-old biophysicist, underlined his arrival as a truly world-class performer when he won the 1982 Commonwealth Games gold medal in Brisbane. The race was run at breakfast time to avoid the peak heat and as millions of Australians watched the action live on television they became convinced their hero de Castella was heading for defeat in his first major championship test.

Tanzanians Gidemas Shahanger – the defending champion – and Juma Ikangaa set off at an absolutely stunning pace. They moved quickly and smoothly through the first mile in 4 min 45 sec. It took tremendous discipline by de Castella not to go with them but he had a race plan and pace set in his mind and was not going to allow anybody to panic him into a change of strategy. Running effortlessly alongside each other, the two Tanzanians pulled further and further away from the chasing bunch in which the tall de Castella was prominent. He knew the course like the back of his hand and was confident the Africans would falter in the last third of the race when the hills of Brisbane would take their toll.

Ikangaa, the African champion and just 18 years old, gradually dropped his countryman and with little more than 6 miles to go had a lead of almost a minute over de Castella who was now making his challenge. Urged on by shouts of 'Go Deek' – his nickname – de Castella started to whittle away at Ikangaa's lead and after almost two hours running and with the finish looming he was just 10 yards behind.

During the next five minutes the lead dramatically changed hands three times as first de Castella and then

Facing page: Robert de Castella wins the 1982 Commonwealth Games marathon championship in Brisbane.

Above: Robert de Castella and silver medallist Juma Ikangaa acknowledge the applause of the crowd after their epic duel.

DE CASTELLA

Ikangaa charged to the front in what had become a battle of wills as much as stamina. Then, with less than a mile to go, the powerful Australian increased the pace and the pressure and this time the little African was unable to respond. With thousands of Australians lining the finish by the south bank of the Brisbane River, de Castella was encouraged to maintain his spurt and he was 12 seconds clear of the gallant Ikangaa as he crossed the line in 2h 09:18·0. For Ikangaa there was the honour of being the first African to break the 2h 10 min-barrier. Fast-finishing Mike Gratton took the bronze medal for England in 2h 12:06·0, just 58 seconds ahead of fourth-placed Scot John Graham.

Ron Clarke, former Australian long-distance ace, summed up de Castella's magnificent performance when he said: 'That has to go down as one of the greatest runs in history. His coolness and composure was just unbelievable. There's no way I would have let those two Tanzanians get away like he did. I would have gone off with them . . . and I would have "died" like they did. Rob paced himself to absolute perfection.'

Despite the mass of runners starting in the 1982 Gillette London Marathon, Hugh Jones (top right) managed to experience the loneliness of the long distance runner before finishing first (facing page) in the shadow of Big Ben.

Britain have uncovered a bright new Olympic hope in Hugh Jones, the winner of the 1982 Gillette London Marathon. The sinewy Jones won in 2h 09:25·0, the fastest time ever recorded in Britain and more than a minute inside his previous best in the Tokyo marathon. Jones surprised everybody except himself by finishing third in the 1981 New York marathon in which Salazar set his new world best time. He prepared for the race by training with top Hungarian marathoners Szkeres Ferenc and Szkeres Janos in Budapest where he has been working on a local government research project. Injury prevented him representing Britain in the 1982 European championships where Dutchman Gerard Nijboer underlined his standing as Europe's No 1 marathon master with a comfortable victory in 2h 15:17·0.

Japan, justifiably proud of their fine traditions in the

Marathon running is thirsty (*above left*) and blistering work (*below*) but victory is sweet as 1978 Commonwealth champion Gidemas

Shahanger (*above right*) will testify. The Tanzanian was also outstanding in the 1982 Brisbane Commonwealth Games.

marathon, are confident of being well represented in Los Angeles, particularly if Toshihiko Seko can produce the form that has carried him to three victories in the exceptionally competitive Fukuoka event and to an impressive win in the 1981 Boston Marathon.

Seko has developed into a world-class marathoner since coming under the wing of famous coach Kiyoshi Nakamura, a retired millionaire businessman who has revolutionised running in Japan with his eccentric but effective teaching methods. Nine of Japan's national track and road records are held by members of his 100-strong private running club. Seko is his star long-distance runner who holds world records at 25 and 30 km.

Under Nakamura's intoxicating influence, Seko reads and studies the scriptures, meditates for hours on end in a Buddhist temple and practices *Zensoho* which, roughly translated, means mind over matter. This mental preparation for races is backed up by an enormous physical output of some 25 miles a day in training. He lives an almost monastic life dedicated to running.

Seko's deadliest rivals, the Soh brothers – Shigeru and Takeshi – are equally committed to marathon running and Shigeru set a new Japanese record at 2h 09:06·0, one of the fastest times in history. Japan can boast at least 20 marathoners close to world class and they are determined to record their first ever Olympic triumph in Los Angeles. Berlin Games winner Kitei Son ran as a member of the Japanese team but was a Korean. The Koreans believe they have discovered another potential Olympic champion in Li Jong Hyon, winner of the 1982 Peking marathon in 2h 14:44·1.

Toshihiko Seko, 1981 Boston Marathon winner and a leader of the Japanese challenge for world supremacy.

Grete Waitz, Norway's queen of the road.

GRETE WAITZ

THE QUEEN OF THE ROAD WHO HAS LED THE WOMEN'S LONG-DISTANCE RUNNING REVOLUTION

WOMEN RUNNERS HAVE HAD to break barriers on and off the road to win acceptance as marathoners who deserve respect and equal rights with the men. The ages-old argument that the marathon was a dangerous endurance test that should be, 'for their own good', prohibited territory for women finally collapsed and expired in New York City on 21 October 1979. That was the day that Grete Waitz, a slightly-built school-teacher from Norway, ran the New York City marathon in a mind-blowing 2h 27:33·0.

Exactly a year but a day earlier Waitz had made her marathon debut in the New York event. She sliced more than 2 minutes off the previous women's best time with a clocking of 2h 32:29·8. Her final placing in a field of 11,000 was one-hundred-and-fourth. There were 999 women and, more significantly, nearly 10,000 men behind her. But it was her performance the following year when she smashed the 2h 30 min-barrier that established once and for all that women and the marathon could get along together very well.

Grete Waitz, born Grete Andersen on 1 October 1953, had done her ground work for the marathon across country, building reserves of stamina and strength with winter runs over fields and rugged terrain that made the roads and avenues of New York City come almost as a relief. She was an international-class track star, specialising at 3,000 metres at which distance she twice lowered the world record in the mid-1970s, before concentrating on long-distance running. Her untapped potential for marathon running was spotlighted when she proved herself the women's No 1 cross country runner by frequently winning the tough IAAF championship. She set women's world records at 10 miles and 20 miles and then brought the world marathon 'record' down to 2h 25:42·0 when completing a hat-trick of New York marathon triumphs on 26 October 1980. It was a time that would have won her the Olympic silver medal behind Alain Mimoun in the 1956 Games.

The eyes of the world were on her again in 1981 as she attempted to win a fourth successive New York marathon but as she sadly surrendered the race because of sore shins a new star was born in the shape of New Zealander Allison Roe, who in just 20 months of marathon running had improved her time by 26 minutes to a world's best in New York of 2h 25:29·0. Among the men who finished behind her was the near-legendary Frank Shorter. It was another giant step forward for women's marathon running.

Roe had taken to marathon running almost by accident. An injury interrupted her preparation for the 1980-81 track season and she entered the Choyso marathon purely for a training spin. She had never before attempted a single run of more than 18 miles and had no intention of finishing the race. 'I wanted to pull out after 15 miles,' she said later. 'But the crowd were full of enthusiasm and they encouraged me to continue.' The secretary from Auckland completed the course at walking pace in a modest 2h 51:45·0 and thought it would be her first and last attempt at the marathon.

Then she discovered that as the first New Zealand woman to finish she had qualified for a trip to the United States and a place on the starting line for the Eugene, Oregon, marathon. She persuaded herself to

The Queens of the Road:

Above: Grete Waitz, who was a world star on the track *(left)* until switching to the marathon and winning the prestigious New York event for a fourth time in 1982 *(right)*.

Facing page: Allison Roe, winner of the 1981 New York marathon in a world's best time of 2h 25:29·0.

Right: Joyce Smith, with the finish of the 1982 London Marathon in sight.

take the event seriously at least for this one race and stepped up her training output from 35 miles to 65 miles a week. She finished a comfortable third in Oregon in 2h 34:29·0 and it encouraged her to enter an all-women's marathon in Tokyo. At 18 miles, she looked poised for victory but then hit 'The Wall', the dreaded physical and psychological barrier that is often the downfall of even the most experienced marathon runners.

'I wondered what had hit me,' Roe said. 'Suddenly I was completely disorientated. All the rhythm went out of my running and I felt so dizzy and heavy legged that I could hardly put one foot in front of the other. It was quite terrifying but somehow, after a road-side stop for a long drink of orange juice, I managed to finish the race.'

It was a brave performance that showed that she had a competitive edge to go with her talent. She completed the course in fourth place, despite badly blistered feet, in a creditable 2h 42:24·0. Two months later she won the Auckland marathon in 2h 36:14·0 and then, in April 1981, beat off the challenge of local favourite Patti Catalano to win the Boston run in 2h 26:46·0. Only Grete Waitz had run the women's event faster.

Married to an American Roe prepared for her challenge against Grete Waitz in the 1981 New York marathon with a series of road races across America. She set a new world record for the women's 20 kilometres and survived attempts to disqualify her from athletics for alleged professionalism. Then she overcame the handicap of tendonitis in her right ankle, ultrasonic treatment clearing the problem just two days before the New York challenge. She ran a perfectly paced race, around 27 min 45 sec for each 5 miles. Greta Waitz had stayed with her for much of the race until finally having to succumb to the shin injury. Roe went away on her own to set a new world record at 20 miles of 1h 50:32·0 and then a final world's best time at 26 miles 385 yards of 2h 25:29·0. There were 112 men ahead of her at the finish but her time was another indication of the progress women marathoners were making.

Born Allison Deed on 30 May 1956, she had not started taking a serious interest in running until the age of 17 after failing to make her hoped-for improvement in her speciality event of high jumping. She was trained for a time by former British track star Gordon Pirie and despite showing a lot of promise in cross country and track races never looked likely to reach top international class.

Then she almost stumbled into marathon running

and she has now opened new horizons for women road runners. 'I think it helps running against men,' she said after her New York triumph. 'Provided women are prepared to put in the sort of training that the men do, I don't think there need be any limitations to what can be achieved, particularly in the big city marathons where the spectators are so helpful with their encouragement and enthusiasm.'

Grete Waitz was back to her unbeatable best in the 1982 New York marathon. She proved she had overcome her injury problems by winning the prestigious event for the fourth time in five years. Her time was 2h 27:14·0. American Julie Brown was the second woman to finish in 2h 28:33·0. 'Grete the Great' later announced that she was retiring from track running to pour all her energies into the marathon. Her ambition is to become the first woman athlete to break the 2h 20 barrier.

Women's marathon running has come a long way since Melopene, a Greek runner, was reported to have set off behind the men in the 1896 Olympic marathon in Athens. She had been refused permission to officially take a place in the race but it is part of Olympic legend that she ran by herself and finished the course in around 4h 30.

The first officially recorded marathon run by a woman was a lone trip over the Chiswick course by Britain's Violet Piercy on 3 October 1926. She was timed at 3h 40:22·0.

It was more than 30 years before any woman tried to better this time because marathon running was considered the exclusive preserve of the male road runners. But American Merry Lepper sparked new interest in the event for women when she clocked 3h 37:07·0 in Culver City on 16 December 1963. The 'record' lasted just five months of the New Year, with Britain's Dale Greig — an unofficial entrant in a race on the Isle of Wight — clocking 3h 27:45·0.

More and more women were turning to marathon running but finding themselves less than welcome on the male-dominated roads. It led to a surge of 'running suffragettes' making their presence felt on the marathon scene. American Roberta Gibb led the way, gatecrashing the famous Boston event in 1966 and 1967, running without an invitation or a number. Each time she finished in around 3h 25.

Katherine Switzer found a way round the problems of entry for women. She applied for a place in the 1967 Boston marathon as simply K. Switzer. Nobody thought of querying her sex and she was given the registration number of 261, dodged the pre-race

Rosa Mota, winner of the first European women's marathon championship in Athens in 1982.

medical examination but then took her place at the start. Boston official John Semple spotted her during the race and tried to physically remove her from the route. But he in turn was unceremoniously bounced out of the way by her boyfriend and bodyguard Thomas Miller who was accompanying her on the run. An alert photographer snapped the shenanigans and women's marathon running got a tremendous publicity boost.

The barriers were being knocked down and America's Road Club staged the first official championship for women in 1970 and Boston welcomed women entrants two years later. Another barrier was smashed on 31 August 1971, when Australian Adrienne Beames broke 3 hours for the first time with a clocking of 2h 46:30·0. This cracked the previous world's best by American Beth Bonner by more than 14 minutes.

There was a three-way struggle for supremacy until Grete Waitz took over as the undisputed Queen of the Roads. Frenchwoman Chantal Langlace, American heroine Jackie Hansen and West Germany's Christa Vahlensieck each lowered the women's world 'record' twice, with the German finally bringing it down to 2h 34:47·5 when winning her national title in Berlin on 10 September 1977

Four months earlier, tiny 5 ft 1 in Chantal Langlace had finished fourteenth in the Spanish marathon open championship at Oyarzun. She was just 14 minutes behind the male winner and what was really significant about her time of 2h 35:15·4 was that she had become the first woman to average under 6 minutes per mile for the full marathon course.

Jackie Hansen has a marvellous long-running record at home in the United States. She lowered the world's

best time for the marathon for a second time at Eugene, Oregon, on 12 October 1975. She clocked 2h 38:19·0, knocking 5 minutes off a previous world's best she had set at Culver City a year earlier. She proved she was a woman of exceptional stamina when she set a new world record for 30 miles at Santa Monica, California, on 9 September 1978. Her time was 3h 45:47·0.

No chapter on the Queens of the Road would be complete without mentioning Britain's Joyce Smith, who has proved that marathon life can begin at 40.

This incredible competitor was 41 when she ran her first marathon, and this after a long and distinguished track career. Coached by her husband Bryan Smith, she won six of her first eight marathons and lowered the British record in five of them. When she won the London marathon in 1981, she became only the third woman to break the 2 hr 30 min-barrier. The following year in the same event she shaved 14 seconds off her previous best time with 2h 29:43·0. On her way to victory in the 1982 London marathon, she handed New Zealand's formidable Lorraine Moller her first defeat in nine marathons.

Joyce Smith has single handed done more for British women's long-distance running than anybody breathing and it was passionately hoped that she could crown her wonderful career by winning the first ever women's European marathon championship on the original Marathon-to-Athens course in the summer of 1982. But she was sadly prevented from competing by a nagging pelvic strain and she had to be content with sitting in a London television studio watching Portugal's Rosa Mota win her first ever marathon in 2h 36:03·0, a time well within Smith's reach.

Even at 44, Joyce was talking confidently of improving her marathon performances. Regardless of whether she is able to recover her peak form, she has already written her own glorious pages in the history of the greatest race on earth – the Marathon.

Hugh Jones and Joyce Smith, leaders of the pack in the 1982 London Marathon.

Robert de Castella, Australia's marathon master.

THE WINNERS

A ROLL OF HONOUR OF THE RUNNERS WHO HAVE WON THE MAIN MARATHON TITLES.

OLYMPIC CHAMPIONS

1896	Athens	SPIRIDON LOUIS *Greece*	2h 58:50·0
1900	Paris	MICHEL THÉATO *France*	2h 59:45·0
1904	St Louis	J. THOMAS HICKS *USA*	3h 28:53·0
1906	Athens★	WILLIAM J. SHERRING *Canada*	2h 51:23·6
1908	London	JOHN HAYES *USA*	2h 55:18·4
1912	Stockholm	KENNETH McARTHUR *S. Africa*	2h 36:54·8
1920	Antwerp	HANNES KOLEHMAINEN *Finland*	2h 32:35·8
1924	Paris	ALBIN STENROOS *Finland*	2h 41:22·6
1928	Amsterdam	BOUGHERA EL OUAFI *France*	2h 32:57·0
1932	Los Angeles	JUAN CARLOS ZABALA *Argentina*	2h 31:36·0
1936	Berlin	KITEI SON *Japan*	2h 29:19·2
1948	London	DELFO CABRERA *Argentina*	2h 34:51·6
1952	Helsinki	EMIL ZATOPEK *Czechoslovakia*	2h 23:03·2
1956	Melbourne	ALAIN MIMOUN *France*	2h 25:00·0
1960	Rome	ABEBE BIKILA *Ethiopia*	2h 15:16·2
1964	Tokyo	ABEBE BIKILA *Ethiopia*	2h 12:11·2
1968	Mexico	MAMO WOLDE *Ethiopia*	2h 20:26·4
1972	Munich	FRANK SHORTER *USA*	2h 12:19·8
1976	Montreal	WALDEMAR CIERPINSKI *E. Germany*	2h 09:55·0
1980	Moscow	WALDEMAR CIERPINSKI *E. Germany*	2h 11:03·0

★Interim Olympics, not officially recognised by the IOC.

THE WINNERS

EUROPEAN CHAMPIONS

1934	Turin	ARMAS TOIVONEN *Finland*	2h 52:29·0
1938	Paris	VAINO MUINONEN *Finland*	2h 37:28·8
1946	Oslo	MIKKO HIETANEN *Finland*	2h 24:55·0
1950	Brussels	JACK HOLDEN *GB*	2h 32:13·2
1954	Berne	VEIKKO KARVONEN *Finland*	2h 24:51·6
1958	Stockholm	SERGEY POPOV *Russia*	2h 15:17·0
1962	Belgrade	BRIAN KILBY *GB*	2h 23:18·8
1966	Budapest	JIM HOGAN *GB*	2h 20:04·6
1969	Athens	RON HILL *GB*	2h 16:47·8
1971	Helsinki	KAREL LISMONT *Belgium*	2h 13:09·0
1974	Rome	IAN THOMPSON *GB*	2h 13:18·8
1978	Prague	LEONID MOSEYEV *Russia*	2h 11:57·5
1982	Athens	GERARD NIJBOER *Holland*	2h 15:17·0

COMMONWEALTH CHAMPIONS

1930	Hamilton, Ont	D. McLEOD WRIGHT *Scotland*	2h 43:43.0
1934	London	HAROLD WEBSTER *Canada*	2h 40:36·0
1938	Sydney	JOHANNES COLEMAN *S. Africa*	2h 30:49·8
1950	Auckland	JACK HOLDEN *England*	2h 32:57·0
1954	Vancouver	JOE McGHEE *Scotland*	2h 39:36·0
1958	Cardiff	DAVE POWER *Australia*	2h 22:45·6
1962	Perth	BRIAN KILBY *England*	2h 21:17·0
1966	Kingston	JIM ALDER *Scotland*	2h 22:07·8
1970	Edinburgh	RON HILL *England*	2h 09:28·0
1974	Christchurch	IAN THOMPSON *England*	2h 09:12·0
1978	Edmonton	GIDEMAS SHAHANGER *Tanzania*	2h 15:39·8
1982	Brisbane	ROBERT DE CASTELLA *Australia*	2h 09:18·0

AMATEUR ATHLETIC ASSOCIATION CHAMPIONS

1925	SAM FERRIS	2h 35:58·2	1957	E. KIRKUP	2h 22:27·8
1926	SAM FERRIS	2h 42:24·2	1958	C. K. KEMBALL	2h 22:27·4
1927	SAM FERRIS	2h 40:32·2	1959	J. C. FLEMING-SMITH	2h 30:11·6
1928	HARRY PAYNE	2h 34:34·0	1960	BRIAN KILBY	2h 22:48·8
1929	HARRY PAYNE	2h 30:57·6	1961	BRIAN KILBY	2h 24:37·0
1930	D. McLEOD WRIGHT	2h 38:29·4	1962	BRIAN KILBY	2h 26:15·0
1931	D. McLEOD WRIGHT	2h 49:54.2	1963	BRIAN KILBY	2h 16:45·0
1932	D. McNAB ROBERTSON	2h 34:32·6	1964	BRIAN KILBY	2h 23:01·0
1933	D. McNAB ROBERTSON	2h 43:13·6	1965	BILL ADCOCKS	2h 16:50·0
1934	D. McNAB ROBERTSON	2h 41:55·0	1966	G. A. H. TAYLOR	2h 19:04·8
1935	A. J. NORRIS	3h 02:57·8	1967	JIM ALDER	2h 16:08·8
1936	D. McNAB ROBERTSON	2h 35:02·4	1968	TIM JOHNSTON	2h 15:26.0
1937	D. McNAB ROBERTSON	2h 37:19·2	1969	RON HILL	2h 13:42·0
1938	J. W. BEMAN	2h 36:29·6	1970	D. K. FAIRCLOTH	2h 18:15·0
1939	D. McNAB ROBERTSON	2h 35:37·0	1971	RON HILL	2h 12:39·0
1946	SQUIRE YARROW	2h 43:14·4	1972	L. PHILIPP *WG*	2h 12:50·0
1947	JACK HOLDEN	2h 33:20·2	1973	IAN THOMPSON	2h 12:40·0
1948	JACK HOLDEN	2h 36:44·6	1974	A. USAMI *Japan*	2h 15:16·0
1949	JACK HOLDEN	2h 34:10·6	1975	JEFF NORMAN	2h 15:50·0
1950	JACK HOLDEN	2h 31:03·4	1976	BARRY WATSON	2h 15:08·0
1951	JIM PETERS	2h 31:42.6	1977	DAVE CANNON	2h 15:02·0
1952	JIM PETERS	2h 20:42·2	1978	TONY SIMMONS	2h 12:33·0
1953	JIM PETERS	2h 22:29·0	1979	GREG HANNON	2h 13:06·0
1954	JIM PETERS	2h 17:39·4	1980	IAN THOMPSON	2h 14:00·0
1955	R. W. McMINNIS	2h 39:35·0	1981	HUGH JONES	2h 14:07·0
1956	H. J. HICKS	2h 26:15·0	1982	STEVE KENYON	2h 11:40·0

THE WINNERS

THE RECORD BREAKERS

The following table reveals how the world's best times for the marathon have been lowered since the standard distance was set at 26 miles 385 yards (42·195 km). Records are not officially recognised for the event because of the disparity in the severity and nature of the courses.

Time	Runner	Course	Date
2h 55:18·4	JOHN HAYES *USA*	Windsor–White City	24. 7.08
2h 52:45·4	ROBERT FOWLER *USA*	Yonkers, New York	1. 1.09
2h 46:52·6	JAMES CLARK *USA*	Brooklyn, New Jersey	12. 2.09
2h 46:04·6	AL RAINES *USA*	Westchester, New York	8. 5.09
2h 42:31·0	FRED BARRETT *GB*	Windsor–Stamford Bridge	26. 5.09
2h 40:34·2	THURE JOHANSSON *Sweden*	Stockholm (track)	31. 8.09
2h 38:16·2	HARRY GREEN *GB*	Stamford Bridge (track)	15. 5.13
2h 36:06·6	ALEX AHLGREN *Sweden*	Windsor–Stamford Bridge	31. 5.13
2h 32:35·8	HANNES KOLEHMAINEN *Finland*	Antwerp (Olympics)	22. 8.20
2h 30:57.6	HARRY PAYNE *GB*	Windsor–Stamford Bridge	5. 7.29
2h 27:49·0	FUSASHIGE SUZUKI *Japan*	Tokyo	31. 3.35
2h 26:44·0	YASUO IKENAKA *Japan*	Tokyo	3. 4.35
2h 26:42·0	KITEI SON *Japan*	Tokyo	3.11.35
2h 25:39·0	YUN BOK SUH *Korea*	Hopkinton—Boston	19. 4.47
2h 20:42·2	JIM PETERS *GB*	Windsor–Chiswick	14. 6.52
2h 18:40·2	JIM PETERS *GB*	Windsor–Chiswick	13. 6.53
2h 18:34·8	JIM PETERS *GB*	Turku, Finland	4.10.53
2h 17:39·4	JIM PETERS *GB*	Windsor–Chiswick	26. 6.54
2h 15:17·0	SERGEY POPOV *Russia*	Stockholm	24. 8.58
2h 15:16·2	ABEBE BIKILA *Ethiopia*	Rome (Olympics)	10. 9.60
2h 15:15·8	TORU TERASAWA *Japan*	Beppu	17. 2.63
2h 14:28·0	LENNY EDELEN *USA*	Windsor–Chiswick	15. 6.63
2h 13:55·0	BASIL HEATLEY *GB*	Windsor–Chiswick	13. 6.64
2h 12:11·2	ABEBE BIKILA *Ethiopia*	Tokyo (Olympics)	21.10.64

2h 12:00·0	MORIO SHIGEMATSU *Japan*	Windsor-Chiswick	12. 6.65
2h 09:36·4	DEREK CLAYTON *Australia*	Fukuoka	3.12.67
2h 08:33·6	DEREK CLAYTON *Australia*	Antwerp	30. 5.69
2h 08:13·0	ALBERTO SALAZAR *USA*	New York City	25.10.81

THE RECORD BREAKERS (Women)

3h 40:22·0	VIOLET PIERCY *GB*	Chiswick	3.10.26
3h 37:07·0	MERRY LEPPER *USA*	Culver City	16.12.63
3h 27:45·0	DALE GREIG *GB*	Isle of Wight	23. 5.64
3h 19:33·0	MILLIE SIMPSON *New Zealand*	Auckland	21. 7.64
3h 15:23·0	MAUREEN WILTON *Canada*	Toronto	6. 5.67
3h 07:26·2	ANNI PEDE-ERDKAMP *W. Germany*	Waldneil	16. 9.67
3h 02:53·0	CAROLINE WALKER *USA*	Seaside, Oregon	28. 2.70
3h 01:42·0	BETH BONNER *USA*	Philadelphia	9. 5.71
2h 46:30·0	ADRIENNE BEAMES *Australia*	Werribee	31. 8.71
2h 46:24·0	CHANTAL LANGLACE *France*	Neuf Brisach	27.10.74
2h 43:54·6	JACKIE HANSEN *USA*	Culver City	1.12.74
2h 42:24·0	LIANE WINTER *W. Germany*	Boston	21. 4.75
2h 40:15·8	CHRISTA VAHLENSIECK *W. Germany*	Dulmen	3. 5.75
2h 38:19·0	JACKIE HANSEN *USA*	Eugene	12.10.75
2h 35:15·4	CHANTAL LANGLACE *France*	Oyarzun, Spain	1. 5.77
2h 34:47·5	CHRISTA VAHLENSIECK *W. Germany*	Berlin	10. 9.77
2h 32:29·8	GRETE WAITZ *Norway*	New York City	22.10.78
2h 27:33·0	GRETE WAITZ *Norway*	New York City	21.10.79
2h 25:42·0	GRETE WAITZ *Norway*	New York City	26.10.80
2h 25:29·0	ALLISON ROE *New Zealand*	New York City	25.10.81

EUROPEAN CHAMPIONS (Women)

| 1982 | Athens | ROSA MOTA *Portugal* | 2h 36:03.0 |

INDEX

PICTURE CREDITS

Allsport: 7, 9 top, 53 top, 58, 60 left, 69, 70, 71, 72, 74 both, 78, 79, 80 bottom, 81, 82 both, 82 bottom, 83, 86 both, 87, 89 bottom, 89 top, 90
Associated Press: 35, 42, 44, 45 top, 45 bottom
BBC Hulton Picture Library: 8, 9, 10 both, 15, 16, 18 bottom, 19 bottom, 20 bottom left, 29 top, 52
Colorsport: 9, 56, 59, 62/63, 62 left, 64, 80 top right, 80 bottom, 86 bottom
Focus on Sports (New York): 7, 76 both, 77 both
Keystone Press Agency: 51
Olympic Press Association: 11, 30 bottom
S & G Press Agency: 31, 32, 38 bottom, 38 top, 42, 44, 48 bottom, 48 top, 49 top
Sports Agency Magazine (Paris): 6, 8 top, 12, 13 both, 14, 17, 18 top, 19 top, 20 both, 21, 22, 23, 24 both, 25 both, 27, 28, 29 bottom, 30 both, 34, 36, 37 top, 37 bottom right, 37 bottom left, 39 top, 39 bottom, 46, 47, 50, 53 bottom, 54, 60 right, 61, 66 left, 68 bottom, 84
Syndication International: 33, 49 bottom, 57, 65, 66 right, 67, 68 left top

BIBLIOGRAPHY

The author wishes to thank Brendan Foster for his contribution to this book. Thanks also to the following authors whose informative books and articles made research work both easier and richly rewarding:

David Martin & Roger Glynn, *The Marathon Footrace* (Charles C. Thomas, Springfield, Illinois); Andy Milroy, *The Long Distance Record Book* (A Road Runners Club Publication); John Hopkins, *The Marathon* (Stanley Paul); Cliff Temple, various articles in the *Sunday Times* and *The Challenge of the Marathon* (Stanley Paul); Neil Wilson, Andy Etchells and Bruce Tulloh, *The Marathon Book* (Virgin Books); the editors of *Sports Illustrated, Track and Field News, Athletics Weekly* and *Running.* Above all to Chris Brasher, of the *Observer,* for bringing the magic of the marathon to London.